The Yeovil Literary Prize
2012 and 2013

An anthology of the best short stories and poems from the Yeovil Literary Prize 2012 and 2013

Yeovil Community Arts Association (YCAA)

Copyright for all text remains with the writers.

All rights reserved. No part of this publication may be reproduced, stored in a retrieval system or transmitted in any form or by any means, electronic, mechanical, photocopying, recording or otherwise, without prior permission in writing of the relevant copyright holder.

Published by YCAA - www.yeovilarts.co.uk

Printed by CreateSpace, An Amazon.com Company

ISBN: 1502426676
ISBN-13: 978-1502426673

CONTENTS

Index of Writers	vi
Introduction	1
The Judges 2012	3
2012 Prizewinners	5
2012 Highly Commended	27
2012 Commended	57
The Judges 2013	95
2013 Prizewinners	97
2013 Highly Commended	117
2013 Commended	153
Biographies	189

INDEX OF WRITERS

Chris Allen *Attack of the Apache* (S 2013)	135
Graham Anderson *Story Time* (S 2012)	8
Chrissy Banks *The Waves* (P 2013)	104
Mike Bannister *Lapidary* (P 2012)	20
Sue Belfrage *Waking* (P 2012)	54
Sharon Black *On the Line* (P 2012)	85
Eve Bonham *I Spy With My Little Eye* (S 2013)	124
J A Brooks *More Than a Butterfly* (S 2012)	80
Beryl Brown *Changing Lines* (S 2012)	30
Michael Casey *The Shape of Rain* (P 2013)	180
Catherine Chanter *Photograph of a Little Girl, Bristol 1960* (P 2013)	134
Siobhan Collins *Stain Removal* (S 2013)	182
Hilary Davies *Examination* (P 2012)	64
Karla Dearsley *Blind Alleys* (S 2012)	86
Ruth Driscoll *For Gracie* (S 2012)	65
Gerard Duffy *Taking Care of Tolly* (S 2012)	50
Gillian Dunstan *Vision* (P 2012)	48
Roger Elkin *Eddie's Mozart Bequest* (P 2013)	155
Suzanne Furness *From Byron to Shelley* (S 2012)	75
Judith Fursland *Shelling Peas* (P 2012)	42
Sandra Galton *With Hindsight* (P 2013)	110
Rose Garland *Exchange Rate* (P 2012)	29
David Grubb *Emily Dickenson's Joke Book* (P 2013)	128
Janet Hancock *Homecoming* (S 2013)	105
John Hargreaves *Speak for Yourself, John* (S 2012)	43
Dennis Harkness *Early Retirement* (S 2013)	147
Bruce Harris *Emily's Derby* (S 2013)	163
Claire Bugler Hewitt *Chawton* (P 2012)	7

Sarah Hilary *My Father's Daughter* (S 2013)	157
Sandy Hogarth-Scott *The Boy* (S 2013)	169
Christopher Holt *The Flags of Our Empire* (S 2013)	119
Tracey Iceton *Dinner for One* (S 2013)	129
Roger Iredale *I-Raq* (P 2012)	74
Sharon Keating *Chanticleer's Egg* (P 2012)	69
Sharon Keating *Shrink* (P 2012)	90
Gill Le Serve *A Stale Bun* (S 2012)	21
Carol Lovejoy Edwards *The Glass Fish* (S 2012)	70
Patricia McCaw *Feeding a Rescued Gannet* (P 2012)	35
Elizabeth McLaren *Lola the Corolla* (S 2013)	111
Dru Marland *Zephyr* (P 2013)	181
Kiran Millwood Hargrave *Grace* (P 2013)	99
Fiona Mitchell *UFO Dad* (S 2013)	175
David Punter *Riau Archipelago* (P 2013)	146
Michael Roe *An Equation for Justice* (S 2012)	91
Emma Seaman *Roses All the Way* (S 2013)	140
Blanche Sears *Negative Equity* (P 2012)	79
Marcus Smith *I Am Human and I Want To Confess* (P 2013)	186
Catherine Strong *Kangerlua* (P 2012)	14
Chip Tolson *Island Summer* (S 2012)	15
Chip Tolson *Everyone is Talking About It* (S 2012)	59
Chip Tolson *Let It Be Anthea* (S 2013)	100
Andrew Tomkinson *The Oxford Companion* (P 2012)	36
Louise Walford *At Prospero's Funeral* (P 2013)	168
Gillian Wallbanks *The Persecution of Peter* (S 2012)	38
Alan Ward *Negative* (P 2013)	162
Louise Warren *Cell Death* (P 2013)	123
Rowena Warwick *Body* (P 2013)	174

Index Code: S – Short Story, P - Poem

INTRODUCTION

Since 2004 the Yeovil Community Arts Association (YCAA) has administered the Yeovil Literary Prize, an international writing competition providing an opportunity for writers, of poetry, novels and short stories, from around the world to gain recognition for their work. Now in its 11th year, the competition has firmly established its place in the literary calendar and several past winners and shortlisted authors have subsequently been published.

The aims of the competition are to promote creative writing and provide opportunities for aspiring writers everywhere. All revenue from the competition is ploughed back into the South Somerset community to sponsor local talent in the study of the arts and to host arts events in the area. The YCAA also participates in the organisation of the annual Yeovil Literary Festival.

The competition category judges commissioned by the YCAA are experienced professionals with literary connections. They may be agents, publishers or successful novelists and poets in their own right.

This is the YCAA's second anthology and contains the winning, Highly Commended and Commended short stories and poems from the 2012 and 2013 competitions. The wide variety of styles and genres it contains gives a flavour of the diversity of entries the competition now attracts from all around the world.

We hope you enjoy it.

For more information about the YCAA and details of how to enter the Yeovil Literary Prize see:

www.yeovilarts.com
www.yeovilprize.co.uk.

2012

THE JUDGES 2012

In 2012, the YCAA invited Sue Freestone as our Short Story category judge. With many years' experience in the publishing world, she had this to say about the shortlist:

'...the themes covered were delightfully varied and the literary techniques employed by the writers also showed a wide and interesting range. The Prize was a pleasure to judge.'

Our Poetry category judge was the eclectic writer of novels, short stories and poetry, Louis de Bernieres. Louis commented that he enjoyed all the poems on the shortlist and also pointed out that one of the Highly Commended poems, Exchange Rate, written by Rosie Garland, revived a holiday memory for him.

He described his First Place winner, the poem Chawton by Claire Bugler Hewitt, as:

'...obscure to anyone who doesn't know about Jane Austen, but if you do, it is absolutely right. It is an exact, simple description.'

To have the poem Kangerlua by Catherine Strong described by him as:

'...possibly the most original love poem I have ever read...' is praise indeed.

The Yeovil Literary Prize

2012 Prizewinners

First

Claire Bugler Hewitt *Chawton* — 7

Graham Anderson *Story Time* — 8

Second

Catherine Strong *Kangerlua* — 14

Chip Tolson *Island Summer* — 15

Third

Mike Bannister *Lapidary* — 20

Gill Le Serve *A Stale Bun* — 21

CHAWTON *by Claire Bugler Hewitt*

1st Prizewinner

It was summer,
but a day in summer is not always warm.

As you left your room,
Did you hope for the strength
for the stairs, for the step to the coach
and the long road ahead;
did you hear, behind you,
the room change its state
from what it had been
to something else?

If you came back,
would you know how the wind
has blown gaps in the floorboards,
warped the wood,
how the things that blew away
were your mother's bed, your sister's half
of the room that you shared, the kitchen, the pond—
and the things that remain
are not your winter boots, nor the piano, nor the chairs,
but collars made of lace,
two silken shoes for dancing, your stitches
in the quilt, the creak of the door,
your letters,
spillikins?

And the thing that took your looks,
your strength and all your thoughts
is named now, pinned on a wall
in a frame, beside your bed,
a captured death's head moth,
all black and white and wrong.

STORY TIME *by Graham Anderson*

1ˢᵗ Prizewinner

Tell us a story!
  Get into bed.
  Tell us a STORY!
  When you're in bed.
  Tell us a story about a manimal.
  It's about a walrus, as a matter of fact.
  What's a walrus, said my-son-John.
  Shan't tell you unless you get into bed.
  Is it a manimal? said Emmaline, Em.
  Could be, I said. It might be, yes.
  Tell us about it.
  It likes bed.
  That's a trick, said my-son-John, climbing up.
  A trick, a trick! said Em, snuggling in.
  The Walrus, I announced.

  The walrus lived by the sea and had whiskers on its face. It swam in the sea and caught fish to eat. When the weather was sunny, it came out of the sea and flopped on the rocks and there it lay, sunning itself and drying its whiskers.

  What was its name?

  First I'll tell you what it looked like and what it did. It looked like a great big fish with fur. It had…

  A fish with fur! A fish with fur! Silly fish!

  But it was not a fish, Emmalo-Em. It was an animal. And its fur was short and very sleek. When it swam in the water it was black and glossy, and when it dried in the sun it was greyish-brown. It didn't have feet, it had two flippers like a frogman, and where you have arms it had two more flippers, and with these two it pulled itself about on the rocks. Flip, flop, flop. And it did a lot of sliding on its tummy because it was a heavy young walrus.

  What was its name?
  Its name was Walrus.
  That's not a name.
  It certainly is.
  It's a silly name.
  Well, that's what Walrus was called. Hard luck.
  How old was he?

Oh, he could have been six, or possibly four. My-son-John looked down at Em and Em looked up at my-son-John. Or he could have been in between. What's in between, Emmy-Em?

After fair consideration Em pushed a hand out of the duvet with all the fingers and thumb spread out.

Is that old for a walrus? said my-son-John.

Just right.

Could it have been a girl as well as boy? said Em.

Just as well.

What did it do?

It had adventures.

Tell us an a-venture. Tell us.

When you lie down properly. One day it got stuck in a cave under the sea.

Why did it do that?

It got stuck in a cave under the sea because a pretty fish swam in and Walrus swam in after.

Did Walrus want to eat the pretty fish?

It might have but I don't think so. It had just eaten eight marmite sandwiches.

That's rubbish, said my-son-John.

No, it found them on the rocks left over from a picnic.

I don't like marmite, said Em.

That's why they were left over. So it can't have been hungry. Perhaps it thought the pretty fish was pretty and wanted to play.

Why couldn't it get out of the cave?

A conger eel came in.

What's a conger eel? said Em.

An eel as thick as my leg and as long as your bed, with teeth.

My bed with teeth, my bed with teeth!

The cave was where the conger lived. It had come home after a morning's swimming and wanted to sleep. It was very sleepy. It had just eaten a bucket of shrimps.

A bucket?

Lying on the sea bed. With shrimps in. It ate the bucket as well.

A bucket!

Conger eels have very strong teeth.

Why did the conger eel eat the bucket? said Em.

Because it had been swimming all morning and swimming makes you hungry.

It does too, said my-son-John, who had done a width last Saturday, his first.

So the walrus couldn't get out. The conger was blocking the entrance to the cave, fast asleep, with its mouth half open and its teeth showing.

What did Walrus do? said my-son-John.

It didn't know what to do. Remember, it wasn't a fish, it was an animal.

Namanimal, murmured Em.

A walrus has to breathe the air, like you and me. It can't stay under water all the time, like fish.

What did it do?

I don't know. If it tried to squeeze past the conger, the conger would wake up. And what do you think would happen then?

It would bite it?

Almost certainly.

What did it do? What did it do? said Em.

It held its breath.

Held its breath?

Held its breath and waited. And so must you. Night-night.

I kissed the brow of my-son-John. I kissed the nose of Emmaline-Em.

That's not fair!

What did it DO?

I'll tell you tomorrow at bedtime.

But it can't hold its breath all night! said my-practical-son-John.

No, but it's quite safe, because the story stops when I turn out the light. There isn't a walrus until we start again. But you can think what you would do, until the story is ready to go on. Night-night. Sleep well.

All right? said my wife, downstairs, turning the pages of a report. Did it go well?

Seemed all right, I said. Something about a walrus.

Oh, good. That sounds safe.

She lifted her face to be kissed.

We ate dinner. We went to bed. In the morning she went off to do more surveying. I went to the office to sell more advertising.

Is the walrus still holding its breath? said Em.

Take your dressing gown off, you'll be too hot.

I'm going to get one with sharks on, said my-son-John.

Rubbish, I said.

Hang it up properly, said Em.

I think the walrus gobbled up the conker eel and just swam off, said my-son-John.

Conger eel. That's rubbish too. Congers are much too big

Big as my bed, said Em, getting in.

Emmalot, I said, you're a clever girl.

See? said Em.

The walrus was holding its breath. It could stay under water for a long time compared to you and me, several minutes in fact. So it stroked its whiskers with its flipper and tried to think what to do. It couldn't squeeze past without waking the conger. It couldn't wait for the conger to wake up and go out again. It might sleep all afternoon.

It had eaten a whole bucket of shrimps, said my-son-John.

Very true, I said.

And the bucket too! said Em. Silly conger.

Sleepy conger, I said. So Walrus swam to the back of the cave to see if there was another way out. Oh, dear.

There wasn't one, said my-son-John. He was really stuck.

There was one. Up in the roof, at the very back. But oh, dear. It was a tiny hole.

How tiny?

You could put your hand through it but not your foot.

Emmaline held her hand in front of her face. She poked a foot out from under the duvet. She lowered the hand and contemplated the foot.

How big is a walrus? she said.

This one was medium. Not big enough to gobble up the conger but too big to escape through the hole in the roof. And time was running out. Its lungs were beginning to hurt.

What's lungs? said my-son-John.

Bags of breath inside your chest.

Yuk, said Em.

Then the walrus had an idea. It remembered the fish.

What fish?

The fish it swam in after, said my-son-John.

Quite right, I said. What else about it?

It was a pretty fish.

Yes. That was Walrus's idea, this pretty thing that it had swum after, into the cave.

What did Walrus do?

It saw the pretty fish swimming at the back of the cave and it paddled up to it very gently so as not to frighten it. And it said, Pretty fish, if we could get out of this cave we could play together in the wide open seas. I can get out, said the pretty fish, through that little hole up there. I can't, said Walrus. The conger eel has come home and it's gone to sleep in the entrance, and I'm stuck, and I need help because I'm running out of breath.

What did the pretty fish say? said Em.

Only tomorrow will tell, I said. Because I've run out of breath for tonight.

That's not fair! said my-son-John.

I kissed a brow and a nose.

Night-night, pretty fishes, I said. Sleep well.

How's the walrus tonight? said my wife, typing notes into her computer.

Stuck in a cave.

Tut. Will you get it out?

Something will emerge, I expect.

So long as you keep it harmless, said my wife, looking round.

I'm not sure you can keep anything from being anything.

Your turn to make dinner, she said, deleting crossly.

Is the pretty fish going to rescue the walrus? said my-son-John, climbing the ladder.

Wait and see. Where's Em?

Here I am! said Em, bursting from under the duvet.

Oh, what a shock. I thought you were lost.

I was hiding in the cave. You were surprised, weren't you?

Would you come and find us if we were lost? said my-son-John seriously.

I wouldn't stop until you were found. Lie down properly, Emma-Lie. What the pretty fish said to the walrus was: Tell me why you called me pretty fish. Walrus said, Because you are small and elusive and shimmer like a rainbow.

What's elusive?

Nice but slippery.

But what happened? said Em.

The fish said, Is that what I am? Fish can't tell what they look like, you see. All they can see of themselves is their tail, sometimes. They don't really know they're there, in reality.

Daddy! said Em.

Sorry. Fine, said the fish. I'll swim through this little hole and I'll wake the conger eel up. Yes, I'll waggle my tail in the sand and she'll come out to look. Then you can escape from the cave and we'll play. You can chase me.

Only pretend, said Em.

First I'll take a good gulp of air, said the walrus, and then I'll chase you all over the sea. Only pretend. But be quick.

It was quite a good plan, said my-son-John, judiciously. Did it work?

You must decide. So the fish swam through the hole and round to the entrance of the cave. It made a big swirly cloud by waggling its tail in the sand, and the conger, with its mouth half open, sucked some in.

Did it wake up?

It sneezed. And then it woke up.

What did it do? What did it do? squealed Em.

It rushed out of the cave, and Walrus rushed after. The conger snapped its teeth because it was cross and frightened and couldn't see what was there. Walrus shot right past and swam up to the surface. It gulped air into its lungs in great big gasps. It was saved.

Hooray! said Emmy-Em.

Where was the pretty fish? said my-son-John.

Inside the conger eel.

No, no!

That's not fair! said my-son-John.

Inside the conger eel, eaten by mistake.

Get it out! Get it out! wailed Em.

Too late. It was bitten to pieces by the snapping teeth. It wasn't the conger's fault. It couldn't see.

Poor little fish!

And the walrus dived back down, and it swam and searched, and it searched and swam, but it never found the pretty fish.

But that's not fair!

Not fair, not fair!

No. Shall we try another story tomorrow? Perhaps we'll have better luck.

And to shut them up, I turned out the light.

You're down early, said my wife, empty-handed for once.

All done, I said. Story ended.

Did the walrus escape?

Yes and no.

What does that mean?

It didn't quite go according to plan.

Oh, John. You didn't put children in this one as well?

I looked away.

She said, We can't torment ourselves for the rest of our lives. It doesn't do any good.

I know, I know. It doesn't do any good.

KANGERLUA *by Catherine Strong*

2nd Prizewinner

I've come further than the wild geese fly,
east of Labrador, north of the Circle
and it's strange to find you here,
among these towering teeth of ice
spat from the glacier, ten thousand
years old; and me, so out of place,
where only the huskies have green eyes,
like you.

My kayak slips through refrigerated air,
parting the brash ice;
pointless to struggle with the current
as we pass those sharp
overhung slits of pale azure,
watching slow wreathes of breath
bequeathed to Kangerlua.

Strange to be together so far north,
where tears cannot fall as liquid
and my blue-ice skin shivers,
endless cold eroding thick seal furs,
layer upon layer, and your smile
still burns a breath-hole through my heart,
even in this frozen land.

ISLAND SUMMER *by Chip Tolson*

2nd Prizewinner

The boys lay back on the heather spotting the trails from airplanes outward bound over the Atlantic. There was no school today and there would be no more school on the island for these two lads. In three weeks they would be weekly boarders at the mainland Academy.

Willie sat up screwing his eyes against the glare across The Sound to the pattern of fishing vessels and beyond to the grey outline of Argyll, his lips stained purple from berries.

'Give us a go of your coke, Andy.'

'Not till lunchtime.'

'You can have a biscuit,' said Willie, 'anyway it is lunchtime,' and he grabbed at the carrier bag.

Andy knew his friend too well and in a flash had rolled out of reach.

'I'm bored.'

'Suppose we could do whatever we wanted, what would you do?'

'We could be a secret gang of spies.'

Andy reached into a pocket and pulled out a piece of paper and the stub end of a pencil. He tore the paper in half and gave a piece to Willie.

'We'll both think up something to do and write it down. We'll have to share the pencil.'

Willie wandered down to the burn to scoop up peaty water. Andy went over to a deserted bothy with no roof.

After the boys exchanged their slips of paper there was silence.

'We can't do this, Willie.'

'We can, my brother says she does.'

'She does what?'

'She has a bath with the window wide open. I heard him saying so to Cronin.'

If Willie's brother had said so to Cronin, then Andy knew it was a fact. On Willie's paper was written the challenge:

"Spy on Mrs. Mermagen in her bath"

Willie was unbelieving of Andy's note. It read:

"Rob a bank."

'But there is no bank,' protested Willie.

'I mean a mainland bank. We'll go to Locharbon. There are lots of banks there.'

'How do you know?'

'My father goes to the bank when he's on the mainland,' Andy had never been to a bank with his father.

Mrs. Mermagen was the Doctor's sister, all the children on the island thought her beautiful. An artist, she came to live on the island a year back and every week she came to the school to teach drawing. She sang songs as she drew while her daughter Abigail played on the floor. There was no Mr. Mermagen. Willie said he'd been murdered. Andy knew he was making that up.

Willie's brother had been on the hill one day looking for a peregrine's nest on the rock face and had seen a shadowy figure through his binoculars at the bathroom window. Willie's brother had whispered this information to Cronin not knowing his young brother was listening.

The doctor's garden harboured the only apple tree on the island a favoured attraction for boys on autumn days. If they were able to climb onto the roof of the old greenhouse they guessed they would be able to see into the bathroom.

The Bank was a bigger problem.

'Why did you put that down?' puzzled Willie.

'I saw this film on the telly. You walk in, give the bank clerk a note and he gives you the money.'

Willie had to admit it didn't sound difficult.

They tossed a two-penny bit. They would go to Locharbon the next day.

The boys were at the pier to watch the ferry dock. Cars drove cautiously off the landing ramp while the gangway was manoeuvred into position by the Piermaster's staff allowing a line of foot passengers to come ashore.

Neither of the boys bought a ticket. They mingled with the crowd struggling onboard with cases while the crew busied themselves getting ready to sail.

As soon as they got to the mainland Andy went to a shop and bought a post card. It had a picture of a highland cow; he said this didn't matter. At the Post Office he used a pen on a chain to write his message in his best handwriting. Willie thought he should have used his left hand and written in wobbly capitals.

The message read:

EXCUSE ME,
CAN WE HAVE TEN POUNDS, PLEASE?
THANK YOU.

The problem was not to find a bank rather which to choose. Andy gripped Willie's arm and guided his companion into the nearest stone-fronted building.

They were at the back of a queue. The lady at the front was telling the man behind the counter she had been on her holiday, but it rained. Willie glanced up, then at Andy clutching his postcard. Everyone was holding a small book, everyone accept them. Above the counter was a sign.

THE ARGYLL PROVIDENT ASSOCIATION

He nudged Andy's arm. 'This isn't a bank,' he whispered.

The queue moved forward Willie stayed rooted to the floor. Andy looked at him then at the sign. They turned and made for the door where an assistant was changing the sign to read: *CLOSED*.

'Remember, boys, early closing today.'

The boys wandered along the street looking into shops, their doors shut, the three Banks and the Provident Society now silent behind stout doors. An amusement arcade was open, but the manager could spot boys without money to spend. He moved them on.

The steamer let its siren blast, Andy and Willie ran to the pier and made it just as the last of the passengers were going aboard.

They spent the crossing on deck. Andy tore up the post card with the picture of the highland cow, letting the scraps spiral down into the ship's wake.

Next day Willie called round to his friend's house. Andy came out with two bacon butties and giving one to his pal they set off at a brisk pace. The boys walked past their old school lying empty as a car came towards them; the Doctor waved.

'Glad he's out,' said Willie. 'We can go in the front gate.'

'No, best go over the wall. Spies never go in the front gate.'

Willie didn't argue.

The boys climbed the wall and with the garden deep in summer growth it was easy to creep unobserved round to the greenhouse. There were panes of glass missing, others broken; a few tomato plants short of water grew inside twisting through an old grape vine.

The bathroom window was open, they could hear singing as a waft of steam came curling out into the sunny morning.

Willie climbed onto a water butt and reached up to the greenhouse roof. Andy went back to the wall to stand guard.

Willie worked his way up the wooden eave taking care to put no weight directly onto the glass panes. At the top there was a pointed finial, he reached out and pulled himself up to the highest point sitting up so his viewpoint was as high as he could make it. Willie heard the bath water released gurgling down the cast iron drainpipe, an arm reached up holding a towel.

Andy watched Willie trying to stand on the greenhouse roof as a large van swept round the corner, stopping in front of the doctor's house, giving several blasts from its horn.

It was the Travelling Bank over on the morning ferry from the mainland. People emerged from houses as Andy whistled a warning to his fellow spy.

Hearing the hooter Mrs. Mermagen looked out of the window. Willie had never in all his life seen so beautiful a sight as Mrs. Mermagen at the window her torso the same sunburned brown as her arms. Willie's mouth fell open and his knees shook.

'Why Willie Campbell, I do declare you're spying on me,' laughed the surprised Mrs. Mermagen lifting her hands to cover her bosom.

People milled round the bank bus. The teller opened the doors and was starting to serve his customers.

Willie lost his balance and with a shattering crash he fell through the greenhouse roof.

Mrs. Mermagen screamed.

The bank was forgotten as the crowd ran from the bus into the doctor's garden.

There was a lot of blood. Cushioned by the vine's encircling boughs, no bones were broken. Prompted either by shock or good judgment, Willie fainted.

By chance the Doctor returned home and making certain there was no serious damage he had the still unconscious Willie carried into the surgery and laid on the couch. Andy crept into the room and saw his friend lying senseless. A warm arm went round his shoulders to comfort him. He turned to find Mrs. Mermagen behind him.

'Is he dead?'

Mrs. Mermagen smiled down. 'No, he's just fainted. He'll be all right.'

The Doctor soon had Willie awake, his cut arms cleaned and bandaged.

'Now then Willie, what on earth were you doing?' demanded the Doctor.

'Oh, I saw it happen,' said Mrs. Mermagen.

Willie thought it best to play faint. Andy looked at his feet.

'He was helping himself to tomatoes when he fell through the greenhouse roof; I told you the greenhouse was dangerous.'

Willie knew at that moment he loved Mrs. Mermagen, even as much as he loved his mother.

Leaving them alone in the surgery the Doctor promised to take the boys home in his car. Andy pushed his hand into his pocket and pulled out something for Willie to see.

'Where did you get that?' demanded Willie.

'From the bank, when they all went to see what had happened.'

'You robbed the bank?'

Andy smiled. He wasn't going to tell Willie the ten pound note had fallen on the ground in the confusion of the accident. After a pause he asked, 'Did you see Mrs. Mermagen in her bath?'

Willie nodded.

It was good being members of a secret gang.

LAPIDARY *by Mike Bannister*

3rd Prizewinner

*In early Spring, out on the hill fort, she starts
the spirit-Hare from his form of bents and fescues;
takes his warmth in her fingers, and places there,
by way of recompense, a sea-worn cockle shell.*

More than an hour we talked that winter night,
while the last light trickled in across your cluttered
bench. You had me mooching through little boxes

for Amber, Lapis, Nacre, Pearl, and Turkey stone,
and then a shuffle of bright filaments, coiled metals
that you might hook and fold to twenty different

chains and sennets, forms numinous, fantastical;
the mythic bird, fronds of a garden in some other world,
a scaled fish, and coral from the deep of distant seas.

I am entranced to learn how you have found
the means to sway their fickle shades with secret
chemicals; how lines and points, out-folded, shape

into space; assume dimension. From what you say
it starts with memory; invention has its own ancestral
chains, like ancient journeys from Allepo to Cathay.

The links divined, a further sense of beauty comes
out of earth-light, and a tribal longing; a jewelled
dream, as if Queen Mab herself had ruled your hand.

A STALE BUN *by Gill Le Serve*

3rd Prizewinner

After the bombing started some months ago food became scarcer and more perilous to find. Tanks patrolled the streets at random intervals, sniper fire could catch you unawares day or night. People stayed barricaded indoors, sometimes still living in homes that lacked a front wall or a staircase, all social contact was aborted. Only the desperate search for the means of survival drove people outside. The town fluctuated between a heavy silence as if a thick duvet was smothering all sound, and a deafening barrage of mortars and shells. Jake had lived on the streets since his mother was no longer able to care for him. His innate cunning had helped him adapt to this harsh way of life but nothing had prepared him for the current situation. In the early days he had easily perfected the arts of scavenging and scrounging by watching others and learning fast. Before the war he had been part of a gang, a strong group of friends who all came from similar backgrounds and thus found solace and support in shared experience. Jake's skill at finding food had soon raised him to the position of leader, a real alpha male. He was expert at searching through bins for that discarded piece of food that was still edible; at judging the precise moment the baker or butcher would dispose of the day's excess. His gentle demeanour and good manners endeared him to strangers when he was reduced to begging, while some local residents allowed him to call regularly at their back doors for hand-outs. He always led his friends to the best pickings.

But now those friends were gone, either killed in the fighting or lost in the upheaval of the fractured town. Just three days ago he had said goodbye to his closest friend, Lennie. They had been forced to venture into an unfamiliar part of town in their never-ending quest for sustenance. Jake, usually the bolder of the two, had been reluctant to go.

"I'm not sure this is a good idea," he said. "We don't know what we may come across over there. Let's stay here for another day and hope our luck changes."

"You know there's nothing here. We've searched and searched," said Lennie truculently.

"But at least we know our way around, we know where to hide when the shooting starts. Once we cross the football ground we haven't got a clue. There may be other gangs there keen to protect their territory who will not take kindly to our trespassing."

"I know, but I'm starving. It's got to be worth the risk. Come on,

Jake, you're usually the brave one."

At this taunt Jake felt guilty and ashamed, he was supposed to be the leader, but he was no longer providing for what was left of his gang. He had known Lennie for years, he was the strong reliable sort, not blessed with much imagination, but willing to follow orders to the letter. So, against his better judgement, they had crossed the football ground and begun to forage on the other side. At first everything went surprisingly well. No other gang materialised and they soon came upon the remains of a market which had clearly been active in recent days as there were still left over scraps of vegetables on the ground. The bombing did not seem to have been so intense on this side as the buildings were in much better shape, a few had clearly been hit but most were still standing intact. As they turned a corner they came upon the find of the day: a half-full pot of cooked rice just left on the pavement. Their hunger drove out any thoughts of caution; they did not stop to question why it had been abandoned in such a way, they were overcome with joy at their luck. They had both had just a few mouthfuls when the shooting started. Gunfire from both sides of the street caught them completely by surprise. Bullets started to ricochet unpredictably in all directions.

They both wanted to stop and finish the rice but their survival instincts told them that would be foolhardy. "Quick, run!" shouted Jake, leading the way down a narrow alleyway. Being in unfamiliar territory they had to guess which way to turn, using their sense of hearing to distance themselves from the shooting. Ten minutes later they were out of breath but all was quiet. They rested for a while, day-dreaming of the unfinished rice.

"I knew this wasn't a good idea, even if we did find food," muttered Jake. "I just sensed it wasn't safe. Let's try and find our way back and hope we can avoid the snipers."

Lennie didn't argue, comfortable in his role as follower he slotted in behind Jake, regretting he had pushed so hard to come to this side of the town, but hunger played with your mind and gave you false courage. Jake confidently led the way, his sense of direction not letting him down and soon they were within sight of the football ground. Best of all they had not heard any more shooting.

"Not far to go," encouraged Jake.

"I'm sorry," replied Lennie. "I should've listened to you, but I was just so hungry."

"Don't worry about it, we're safe now."

They had just entered the football ground from the western side and were making their way down an aisle when a single shot rang out. It bounced off a metal hoarding at the back of the top row of the stand and caught Lennie in the stomach. He faltered then fell to the ground.

"Lennie, what's the matter?"

"I'm hit. I can't move, it hurts too much. I need to lie here and rest."

Jake looked around, he could not see any movement, but he knew they needed to get under cover.

"We must get under the seating where there's some protection. Can you just crawl a few yards?"

Lennie made a desperate effort to move, Jake trying to help him by gently tugging on his shoulder. He managed to get under the cover of the seating then collapsed. Jake could see blood oozing from the wound, he knew it was serious, but was determined to try and keep up Lennie's spirits.

"You'll be all right, it looks worse than it is. You just need to rest a bit. I won't leave you."

There was no one Jake could call on for help, so he lay down next to Lennie hoping the proximity of his body would give him comfort. The sun was going down quickly now, soon night would fall and the temperature would drop considerably. On their home streets they usually managed to find some old cardboard boxes to sleep in, or they would curl up against the bricks of the baker's chimney which were still warm from the day's work. They would just have to make the best of it where they were. As the sky darkened Lennie started to slip in and out of consciousness, he was still losing blood. Jake kept talking to him, tried to engage him in conversation, to play their favourite game, 'Do you remember when?', but Lennie was unable to respond. For the first time in his tough life Jake felt inadequate, he didn't know how to make his friend better, he was letting Lennie down. Lennie had always looked up to him, obeyed his orders, ever faithful. Jake curled up even closer to him hoping that his own body heat would help him survive the night, but a cold fear gripped his chest, he knew he was going to lose him.

Jake slept fitfully, and when the first rays of daylight penetrated their hiding place he knew instinctively that Lennie was no longer alive. He had no choice but to leave his body there, he had to set out on his own. He made his lonely way back to his own district without hearing further sounds of gunfire. In fact everywhere was sinisterly quiet. He saw the occasional person trying to find food for his family, but most of the shops had been looted long ago and there was little if nothing left. A rare shop remained open but their supplies were nearly exhausted and they would be forced to close soon. When the bombs had first landed Jake and his gang had welcomed the sudden bounty that doorless premises provided, little did they appreciate then how serious the situation would become.

Jake's own hunger tore at him from the very pit of his stomach, giving off a dull repetitive rumble like a goods train coming down the tracks. He must find something to eat, he had had nothing since those few mouthfuls of rice. He looked round at the changed landscape that was now unrecognisable as the town of his youth. Contorted buildings and chasms of bizarrely angled concrete filled his vision. He felt weak and light-headed but he forced himself to move on, knowing his life depended on it. On a fruitless expedition the day before he had cut his foot on a piece of buckled metal. It wasn't a deep cut, but was painful enough to make him limp.

Covering ground he had already covered in the previous days, but hoping a vain hope for success he came to the back of an old bakery where the owner had always treated him kindly. There was no one about. The door hung open on one hinge, the ovens were cold, the shelves empty, but Jake felt sure there might be something he had missed earlier. He searched around – nothing. A sense of failure lay heavy on his heart, but he still persisted. Peering into a dark corner he suddenly noticed a pale white lump half hidden by the leg of a table. This part of the room seemed quite damp and at first Jake thought it was just some fungus growing there. But on closer inspection, he realised it was actually food. A stale bun! Dry, crumbling, tasteless, but food. Unable to hold back, he gulped it down voraciously, not having the sense to eat it slowly, make every crumb last as long as possible. It wasn't much, but it would help, maybe even be a life saver.

The heat of the day was starting to become oppressive so he decided to rest in the bakery for a while and lay down on the cool tiled floor. He knew he wouldn't be able to stay for long, the pursuit of further nourishment would drive him on, but for now he was content. On top of which his cut was becoming more painful, exacerbated by the heat. With a sigh Jake leant forward and started to lick his paw.

**The
Yeovil
Literary
Prize**

2012 Highly Commended

Rose Garland *Exchange Rate*	29
Beryl Brown *Changing Lines*	30
Patricia McCaw *Feeding a Rescued Gannet*	35
Andrew Tomkinson *The Oxford Companion*	36
Gillian Wallbanks *The Persecution of Peter*	38
Judith Fursland *Shelling Peas*	42
John Hargreaves *Speak for Yourself, John*	43
Gillian Dunstan *Vision*	48
Gerard Duffy *Taking Care of Tolly*	50
Sue Belfrage *Waking*	54

EXCHANGE RATE *by Rosie Garland*

At the next table, four Germans order tea. One glass each.
They raise their hands, palms shoved forward, say *no sugar*
in precise Arabic. The tea-boy scratches his ribs, shrugs.
Tea without sugar? A rainy season without rain.
A homecoming unsweetened with greetings, hand-holdings.

They sip the bitter brew. The tea-boy poises
with a spoon: any minute now
they'll spit it out, change their minds.

When they're done, they get the bill: one hundred piastres,
Enough to buy a stick of chewing gum in Düsseldorf.
The haggling starts. *Sugar is expensive*, they say.
We did not have any, they say. *We should pay less*.
Each word correct and in its proper place.

CHANGING LINES *by Beryl Brown*

I was dozing when the train jerked to an abrupt halt. The newspaper slid off my lap and, as I fumbled around on the filthy floor to retrieve it the lights flickered, went out for a second, then recovered their unforgiving glare.

The train was silent. I was hungry and tired and hoped we hadn't broken down. I'd read the paper and struggled with the crossword at the beginning of the journey and my bored gaze now wandered over the shabby seats and littered floor. Then my eye was caught by a book lying under the next seat. How had I missed it when picking up the paper?

Stretching my shoulders, I looked at my reflection in the window against the dark night. How would someone outside see me? Fortyish, receding, an air of responsibility, probably a lawyer - which is true - or, heaven forbid, an estate agent. An predictable boring man with a boring life. Surreptitious glances at other reflections revealed only a couple of fellow commuters further along the carriage: one asleep and one tapping earnestly on a laptop.

After a few minutes more tedium, I reached out with my foot and dragged the book over. It had an old fashioned matt blue binding with the title, "The Antidote", in gold lettering on the spine. I opened it and was surprised to discover crisp white leaves and, as I flicked to chapter one, the unmistakable new book smell that enticed me to read on.

The book was just to my taste, a thriller, and after a few paragraphs I was engrossed in the riveting story of a hero who became consumed in a complex plot to save his home and family but without alerting them to the danger.

So absorbed was I that when someone coughed beside me I jumped and took a few seconds to recall my whereabouts. Thinking this person might be the owner of the book I quickly stuffed it down beside the armrest and looked up innocently. It was the man with the laptop.

'What do you think's causing this delay? Shouldn't we do something?' He had a sharp nose and a spiky ginger moustache and reminded me of a hamster I'd had as a boy.

'Oh, I don't think so,' I was anxious to be rid of him, 'it's not been that long.'

He looked at me curiously, whiskers bristling.

'An hour and fifteen minutes.'

'What..? Oh well, I expect we'll be on the move soon.'

I opened the book before he had even moved away. It was brilliant and I was half way through already. The plot was enthralling and the characters so well drawn I felt they were life-long friends. My heart went out to Dillon, the protagonist, who was now trapped and had to escape before saving his family. I looked for the author's name but it wasn't on the cover and I couldn't be bothered to search inside, I just wanted to know what happened next.

The lights flickered again and the train jolted into life. I glanced across at the hamster man. He pointedly ignored me. Too bad, my station must be coming up soon and I had to finish the book.

The tension was so great I couldn't bear to miss a word so it was taking a long time to read. Both the other passengers had left the train by the time we approached my stop. I was perching right on the edge of my seat, backside barely in contact and leaning forward as if to slip-stream to the end of the story. I had just begun the final chapter when the train pulled into the platform.

Grabbing my coat from the overhead rack I dropped the book into my briefcase, but not without a twinge of guilt. Solicitors are not supposed to steal but leaving the book unfinished simply wasn't an option.

I jumped off just as the train started to move on. My feet hit the ground hard and the impact jarred up my legs making me stumble.

'Nodded off, sir?' the station master asked as he slammed the door.

Even in the dim lamplight I could read his expression and almost feel him sniffing my breath.

'Something like that. Goodnight.'

I hurried out into the road. I was desperate to know what happened at the end of the story and started to jog. My neighbour, Bob, heading for the pub looked startled. I wasn't the kind of man who ran anywhere.

'What's up, Phil?'

I slowed a fraction. He wouldn't understand the truth. 'Got to catch someone on the phone'.

'No mobile?' he shouted.

I waved a hand and powered on. My heart was pounding and breath was rasping in my throat. Somehow it was impossible to slow up. Feeling I was about to collapse, and cursing myself for not having joined a gym, I forced my pace to a fast walk. I refused to think about the book for about a minute, but then found myself jogging again.

I burst through the front door, threw my coat on the sofa and yanked open the briefcase. The book wasn't there.

I shook the bag upside down. Papers, pens and a long lost propelling pencil cascaded over the settee, some rolling off to be kicked away in my frantic search. Again and again I returned to the empty case scouring every inch and frantically ripping out the lining. Still no book.

I tried to rationalize the situation. What was making me act like someone deranged? I was a lucid balanced person and had only lost a book.

I poured myself a glass of malt and downed it in one, the peaty flavour that I normally savoured completely lost on me. All I could think of was Dillon and whether he'd escaped and got his family safely away.

I found myself in the kitchen searching a drawer and, finding a torch, checked the garden path. Nothing. I began to retrace my steps to the station flashing the light right and left.

'Are you all right, Sir?' The station master looked at me warily.

'Have you seen a book? Blue cover, old looking, called "The Antidote"?'

'A book? No, sir and we've just swept the platform. Did you leave it on the train, you were asleep after all.'

'I wasn't bloody asleep. I was reading it. I put it in my briefcase and it's not there now.'

He glanced around nervously. There was no-one in sight.

He spoke slowly and deliberately, elongating the syllables, 'Look sir, we can ring the lost property office in the morning. Best go home now, it's freezing and you've no coat.'

He was right. I began to shiver violently as I walked back checking every shadow.

At last, exhausted, I crashed on the sofa with another large whisky. I'd no appetite and couldn't even be bothered to go upstairs. I pulled my coat over me and fell into a dream-filled sleep in which I was tormented by a hand waving a book from the window of a moving train.

The next morning I rang in sick, the first time in fifteen years, then went to the station and searched again. I stood over the station master when he rang the lost property office. Snatching the receiver from him I berated the clerk at the other end who insisted nothing had been found on the train.

My life over the next few months became one of interminable searching. Before I began "The Antidote" quest I had disregarded second hand bookstalls and had hardly ever been inside a charity shop. Now I established a routine, my "round" as I called it, of stalls and shops and even learnt to ignore the smell of old clothes. Every day there were new books to be searched through and each day began with hope which changed to increasing disappointment as I got to the lowest shelf, or bottom of the last box.

Fruitless hours were spent scanning every search engine for "The Antidote". When that failed I rang bookshops. None of them could find the title and I couldn't give them the name of the author or publisher. The local librarian took to hiding in the back room whenever I entered the building.

My senior partner delivered an ultimatum, which I ignored. I had no time to bother with the rat-race. My charity shop searches however, bore fruit of a kind; the staff at the local shops got to know me and I was often provided with a coffee in exchange for legal advice on a house purchase or how to deal with a difficult neighbour. It was during one of these sessions I was offered the opportunity to provide the charity with regular legal surgeries at its shops throughout the region. Of course, this enlarged my searching area as well as providing an income which covered my meagre needs.

The sessions become very popular. I was getting a name for helping people in difficulty and when I finished a surgery one afternoon, I was having a final search of the book shelves when I bumped into a woman scrutinising every volume.

'Excuse me,' I said as my eye was caught by a blue book with gold lettering. I reached to grab it at the same time as she did. My good manners did not override my desperation but she had hold of the book and I couldn't risk damaging it.

'Is it "The Antidote?' I asked, my voice a high squeak.

She stared at me and slowly revealed the title. *"Little Women"*. My heart sank, as usual.

'You know "The Antidote"?' she asked, her face a mask of disbelief.

She was about my age, slim and attractive in an understated way.

'Yes.. and you?'

'I've spent three years trying to find it.' She replaced *"Little Women"* on the shelf. 'I found a copy on a train but didn't have time to finish it. I lost it when I got off, although I know I'd zipped it in my handbag.'

We decided to continue our chat elsewhere and ordered a pot of tea in a dingy café with grey net curtains.

Julie explained that, like me, she was driven. After abandoning a humdrum accountancy career, her search had encouraged her to begin dealing in rare books. She loved the life and visited auctions and boot fairs as well as charity shops.

'Of course my priority is to find "The Antidote". I dread to think how much I would pay if I discovered it in an auction lot.'

I don't think either of us could really believe someone else knew of "The Antidote". We discovered our obsession had begun on the same train, and roughly the same seat, but three years apart.

'I went to the railway lost property office and insisted on examining their records,' Julie told me.

She went on to say that there had been another Antidote enquiry about five years before hers. 'There were some notes written alongside the entry because the man had made such a fuss. Same as us, train broke down and he hadn't finished the last chapter before he got off.' She poured more tea. 'The clerk remembered him because he later saw him on TV. Apparently he'd given up a Harley Street practice to set up a charity for kids with terminal diseases – giving them dream holidays and so on.'

I was digesting this as she added, 'There's a funny thing about him too, he described "The Antidote" as the best nautical story he'd ever read.'

'Nautical?'

'Yes, isn't it odd? He must have been confused, there was no mention of the sea in the book was there?'

'No, definitely not. Not in the Outback, but it was certainly the best thriller I've ever read.'

'Thriller? It was a Parisian romance.'

FEEDING A RESCUED GANNET *by Patricia McCaw*

My manager hands me a fish with 'Mind the beak!'
but the eyes trap me, adrift as the Arctic.
He's blown off course, no pain, no break,

they claim, but I see something tragic.
Blue blazes me, rim within rim.
He lunges, jabs, denies he's sick,

still claiming his right where he can't be king.
After I crossed the Irish Sea
I lay on the Galloway Rhins

watching gannets patrol, alert and free,
fierce border guards with tilting wings
to dive for fish, repel the returnee

who migrate, re-seek, and spin in rings,
doomed never to find the landing strip.
I nod at the bird—he bows and sings,

gapes, surrenders. Brine soaks my lip.

THE OXFORD COMPANION *by Andrew Tomkinson*

No space in this city, amongst the undergrowth,
thistled thickly with chimneys and spires.
Not dreaming, just resting on the rooftops; needles
that would put the evening to sleep.

Inked into the shadows cast by overgrown stone
lurk a limbo of orphaned muses.
Those not yet fostered drift in clusters through the streets
in dark gowns, the floating ghosts of crows.

They glide across courtyards under a gargoyle leer,
the pavement a gravel of spent quills.
Crowd around the Camera, lenses blink like eyes;
pictures taken cannot be returned.

No room at the Eagle, the Lamb, the Madding Crowd
of ogres, jagged shoulders and orcs.
Scratched into the tables, one thousand years of names;
cannot even write mine on the page.

Traffic jams the Cherwell, drivers stab at the air,
arms stirring the tarmac with long poles.
At the Cambridge end sits, perched, each twit with his twoo;
perfect human symmetry of love.

Full, too, by the Folly, where swans beg at the bench
and rowers pass in twos, fours or eights.
Easels stand crammed around abandoned Wonderlands,
snatching at the scraps of what remains.

Even in the fields, hedges a barbed-wire frame,
rusted nibs poke up through cobbled soil.
A picture must exist of every inch by now,
a poem composed from every bench.

It seems each tree has been the scene of someone's dream,
and now it belongs only to them.

Each thought, each glance, each walk by the canal now seized,
claimed in paint and hung on someone's wall.

And all the space there seems to be is really filled
with the stomping footsteps of dragons,
with the faded litter of war; wands, rings and swords,
with the echo of a lion's roar.

Ink falls like rain from every other pen but mine.
I let go, it tumbles off the desk.
I let go, under the spires. No space for angels
to land on Oxford's prickly back.

THE PERSECUTION OF PETER *by Gillian Wallbanks*

Mr Carter, our History Teacher, tells us that young men were unjustly shot in World War 1 for cowardice. I'd definitely be one of those, but I suppose my death would be deserved because I am a coward.

I look at my watch, tenth time in ten minutes I reckon. I just wish Mrs Webb, the biology teacher, would stop yakking. One minute to three fifteen. Please, please, *please*, let the school bell ring exactly on time. If teacher let us out even a half a minute early, or exactly the moment the bell sounds, I'm safe. Any time after that, I'm in dead trouble.

Yesss, twenty seconds to go and the best sound in the world echoes around the school.

I collect my pens, pencils, books from the desk, ram them into my school bag, and run for the door like an Olympic sprinter.

"Peter Gold, why are you rushing off again so quickly?" Mrs Webb yells as I wrench open the door. I don't answer, speed's dead important.

I hurry along the corridors to the front entrance; kids keep pouring out of their classrooms and getting in my way. I push past them although when I reached Form 12b, the boys are bigger than me, so I'm careful. Bump into them and you could get a thump. The girls are just as bad, but over the last six months, I've got well good at dodging round them.

At the front door, I glance at my watch that I keep dead accurate. Well, this is the third watch I've kept exact in the last six months. They nicked the other two. One I had from Grandma for Christmas and the other one I got for my birthday in February because I made out I'd lost the first one. I don't want them getting their filthy hands on this one.

One minute and twenty seven seconds past three fifteen and I leg it out of the school grounds, turn left up London Road, dodge round the back alley behind the sweet shop and I'm out of sight. Hopefully they haven't twigged they miss me if I get out of school on time. Then I leg it over the playground, dodging round all the kids who're ambling along, no worries; lucky things. Why am I picked on?

By the time I hit the alleyway, I'm usually out of breath. Not today, must be getting fit, all this running. I check the time again, twenty five past three. Five minutes and I can catch the early bus, and then I'm definitely out of harm's way. They don't live on my estate, so once I'm on the Number 17, I'm OK. When I'm in the bus queue, I'm pretty safe too. I've learned that if there are a lot of people, you can crouch down and mingle in, then you're not noticed between the chattering woman and all the other kids loaded down with bulky satchels.

I can't get it out of my head. Why me, why do they pick on me? It started the day Mr Donahue, the Head Master, read out my test results at the end of the Autumn Term to the whole school at Morning Prayers and Assembly. I'd scored 95% in maths, 96% in science, 89% in English, and the other marks were pretty decent. They got me as I left school that day. They said I spoke posh and I was a ******* swot. I'm not a swot or posh; we live in a tiny terrace house.

I had £7.45 on me. I was going to buy dad a Christmas present on the way home from school. They pulled open my school bag, found the dosh hidden in an inside pocket and took it. That's when they took the watch Grandma gave me, ripping it off my wrist. They threatened that if I told anyone, they'd beat me up and set fire to the house. Twisting my arm, Aaron Turner gave me a Chinese burn and made me tell them Grandma's address. She lives just round the corner and they said they'd torch her place as well if I grassed. I must be some sort of coward if I can't stick up for myself.

That was just the start of it. I have to pay them my pocket money every week. If I don't bring it they beat me up. They ripped the pocket from my blazer once. Got Grandma to sew it back on. Made out I'd torn it off on the swings in the park.

Usually no one's home when I get home. If Gran's arthritis isn't playing up, she sometimes comes round. Dad gets home about six o' clock. I didn't used to mind. Dad always said to get my homework done and then the time would go quicker. Anyway, in the summer, if I've finished my homework, I'd go and play on the green just down the road. Billy Carter and Paul Mullins and I used to kick a ball about. I daren't go out now in case they come and set fire to the place. Dad asked me why I didn't go out to play anymore, but I just made out I was bored with kicking a ball.

The bus comes on time. I feel good; they're nowhere in sight. Only takes twenty minutes to get to my estate. I see Billy and he asks me if I'm going to play footy? I say no, got homework. He tells me I'm turning into a goody goody. I'm fed up as I go into the house. Billy and I used to be good mates, have a real laugh together, now he thinks I'm a twat. Twat and a coward. But I can't take no chances that they'll torch the house.

I hurry into the garden shed and check under the bench. I've hidden some rope there where dad won't find it. I keep thinking about getting a ladder, and tying the rope to the ceiling, then round my neck and jumping. I feel the rope, well rough and strong. That would solve everything, but that's just being a coward too. Still, that's all I am, a damn coward. Maybe I'll do it one day if I get brave enough, ha ha! I'm scared it'll hurt a lot and I don't want to upset dad and Grandma.

Back in the house, I'm just getting my homework out of my bag when I hear a key go into the front-door lock. My stomach goes all funny. It can't be dad, too early. It's Susie, his girl friend. She's alright. I'm surprised, because in comes Tommy as well, her eldest kid, he's fifteen. He's well tall, nearly two metres I reckon.

"Just getting the casserole on for your dad," she says. "Fancy a cuppa?"

I nod. Tommy goes into the living room and switches on the telly. I watch as she fills the kettle.

"You OK, Peter?" she says.

"Yeah."

She's quiet; then she suddenly says. "I've been coming here for nearly a year. I always thought you quite liked me. Is that right?" I nod. "Good. Just lately though, I've noticed you're real withdrawn. Not in trouble, are you?"

"No." Hope I'm not going red, my cheeks feel like they're burning.

She turns round and looks me straight in the eyes. "You're not on drugs, are you?"

"No way. Drugs is for dick-heads," I say. Then I realise what I said. "Sorry 'bout the swearing."

She makes the tea; pours it. We sit at the breakfast bar like we normally do. Dunk ginger biscuits in our tea.

"Not being bullied, are you?"

I didn't know what to say at first. "No, course not." I look down and drink my tea.

"You don't have to put up with anything like that. You can always tell someone, you know. You're dad's busy, but tell him, he'd want to know. Or tell me, I'll get something done about it."

Yeah, like she can stop them torching our house or Grandma's when she's not there.

"I'm fine. There's nothing wrong." I can't let her know I'm scared, she'd think I was a right woofter.

She gets this casserole thingy ready and puts it in the oven. She calls for Tommy; they gotta go.

"Be back about sixish," she calls back to me as she leaves. I think I fooled her. Tommy walks into the kitchen and chucks his Mars wrapper into the bin. As he leaves, he says, "If they get up close, knee 'em in the googlies, works every time." Then he goes. I stare after him, my heart's pounding well hard. He must know I'm a coward.

Two days later, they get me again. The bell went a bit late and I just get round the corner from the school. They're waiting. They spread out across the pavement, I can't get past. James Cornwall walks up to me. He grabs my wrist and pushes up the sleeve of my blazer.

"Whad'we have here? Hey look, guys. Another watch for our collection." He leans down, right in my face.

I hear Tommy's voice, real clear, like it's inside my head. I do it; I push my knee up real hard into his groin. He looks all amazed, his eyes go all big and poppy; then he goes, "Aaagh," and falls on his knees. The other two look surprised and rush forward.

"You little *******," Aaron Turner yells. "I'll kill you." He gets out a knife, waves it in my face. "I'm gonna cut your nose off for doing that to my mate."

He brings up his left fist, swings back his right arm with the knife. *I'm gonna die!*

Suddenly he's twisting round, screaming 'aaagh'.

It's Tommy. "Scarper," he yells. He twists Aaron's arm again, telling him to drop the knife. He wouldn't, until Tommy kicked him in the back of his knee. I kick the knife away.

Danny Cox runs off, but Cornwall wades in.

"No way I'm leaving you," I yell to Tommy.

We had a right punch up. Tommy got a black eye, a split lip, and my nose bled down my shirt. We won though; they just run off in the end.

Tommy throws the knife in the river; then we walk to the bus stop. "I knew something was going on," he said. "You were well brave. They're bigger than you. How old are you anyway?"

"Fourteen... nearly."

"Yeah, well... good fight, Bro." He gives me a high five and turns off down Shipton Lane to walk to his house. I catch the Number 17 bus.

I feel well good. I get home and head straight to the shed and bung the rope in the dustbin. I wash the blood out of my shirt the best I can and chuck it in the wash basket, hoping dad won't notice what's left of the stain. Dad comes home and I make him a cup of tea.

I may not be a hero, but I'm not a coward either. No ones gonna torch my house, or Gran's, and I'm keeping this watch for good. After dinner, I go and play with Billy and Paul.

SHELLING PEAS *by Judith Fursland*

Touching your cool, smooth,
water polished skin,
pressing my thumb gently
on the proud pout
of your mouth, I
carefully part your lips.
Hearing the soft pop
of escaping breath,
seeing the sweet, green, pearl sphere
at the end of a string
of small green pearls.
Tasting the sweet, sweet
greenness of early summer
and the promise of more to come.

SPEAK FOR YOURSELF, JOHN *by John Hargreaves*

Being theatrical, I'll start with our dramatis personae:

Geraldine is a senior committee clerk at my local council. She was conveniently on annual leave throughout the recent scandal of the councillor and the schoolgirl.

Noah is a graduate trainee with the council. He is eager to please but politically naïve, and doesn't realise that he is the obvious fall guy.

Josh is the artistic director of Ploughdown theatre company.

Oscar is Head of Music and Dramatic Arts at Valeston School and Sixth Form College. That's me, your narrator. And since I have the conch (reference Lord of the Flies, GCSE perennial), I will add that I have reached the point where my flair for teaching theatre and my dislike for politicians telling teachers what to do, while claiming the opposite, are in combustible combination.

Now the location:

The four of us are sitting in a cubicle in the corner of the lobby of our council's headquarters. Troubled life is displayed before us, queuing in front of main reception. We are in the 'private interview chamber' which has glass on all sides. The four chairs and small table fill the cubicle. It is fortunate that the door, also predominantly glass, opens outwards. Perhaps this private chamber was constructed in reaction to 9/11, as a way of keeping visitors out of the belly of the building; perhaps in a flurry of good intention when the council discovered the notion of customer service. In either case, the privacy refers to sound only. Visually we couldn't be more on show. I may be able to craft sound and sight into a metaphor for the Leader of the Council and his problem with the schoolgirl.

Geraldine is leading a preliminary enquiry. She will report to the Head of Legal Services.

"Perhaps you could start, Noah," she says to the young graduate trainee, "by explaining to me the thinking behind this **SPEED DATING** event you created." She projects in bold capitals the two words which describe the start of the affair.

"Not my idea originally," he says, as if this would surprise anyone. "The Local Government Association came up with it years ago, after Sex in the City and all that. Political Speed Dating. Good PR for Local Democracy Week. Bring Councillors and young people together in a way neither group would find so intimidating. Open a dialogue. Councillor Evergreen became interested when his daughter Jessica was elected chair of the sixth-form student committee at Valeston. He said the two of them could make it happen brilliantly, and that it would cast his unpopular administration in a more human light."

"And what exactly did happen?"

"We had desks back-to-back in pairs, with a little elbow room between; twelve hand-picked councillors briefed to call them 'young people' not 'children'; and twelve hand-picked young people briefed to call them 'councillor', not 'sir' or 'man'."

"Boys AND girls?"

"Almost all females actually. I hadn't taken account of a United game playing at the same time. Mostly Jessica's clique. And almost all male councillors, naturally. I rang a bell and the pairs started talking at once. The noise generated lots of energy which overcame nerves and rather surprisingly ensured privacy."

"What did they talk about?"

"You name it… everything from vending machines in the sixth form common room to the need for a refuge for battered women."

Geraldine makes a note on her notepad.

I say, "This is the safety catch, which is always released with an easy flick of the thumb. And please do not let me see anyone using his finger. You can do it quite easy if you have any strength in your thumb."

Josh rolls his eyes.

"Sorry?" Noah says.

"Naming of Parts. Henry Reed. The text's on Google. Plus a film version by Robert Bloomberg which won the Student Peace Prize at the 13th annual American Film Festival, 1972." This is my reaction to Michael Gove's diktat that all schools should have a Combined Cadet Force. I'm setting the poem to music with my lower sixth. We're making an opera. The Head of PE is doing the CCF thing. I wave my arm to indicate the council's customers outside our investigative bubble and recite: "The blossoms are fragile and motionless, never let anyone see any of them using their finger."

"How do you know what they talked about?" Geraldine asks, unmoved.

Noah says, "Councillor Evergreen told me the council had paid for a new sound lab at Valeston School just before the cut backs."

"So you taped the conversations."

"It's all digital actually. We got everyone's permission. After five minutes I rang the bell again and the young people all moved along one, for their next date. Then again. Twelve times in all. The bell was a nice touch – apparently they don't ring them in schools any more. Then we had a break for refreshments."

"Any alcohol?"

"Strictly tea and coffee. But still everyone was buzzing. They all wrote down the three 'dates' they most wanted to re-visit and I did some quick permutations. They went back for follow ups. And then we had a wash up and de-brief."

"This is the lower swing swivel," I recite. "And this is the upper swing swivel, whose use you will see, when you are given your slings."

Geraldine looks at me like a disapproving aunt. The air is getting thick. Her nostrils widen briefly and I wonder if she has identified me as the one who didn't shower this morning.

"Can we open a window?" I ask.

"I'm afraid not," Geraldine says. "Except metaphorically."

I point to a little device up in the corner: "Is that where they squirt in the poison gas, when you've got everything you want from us?"

"It's CCTV, as I'm sure you are aware, Oscar."

Josh is aware that I am deeply upset that my school is about to become an academy. I am aware that the council leader is attempting to blame my department for his schoolgirl scandal. Noah is aware that academies don't have to give a damn what local authorities say. I am aware that the real world doesn't work like that.

"Moving on," Geraldine says. "How did you become involved, Josh?"

Josh has worn a tie especially for the meeting. He slackens the knot and runs a finger round the inside of his shirt collar. "It's like a torture chamber. Isn't there some health and safety rule?"

"Actually, there's a statutory minimum temperature for council offices," Noah says, "but no maximum. They warned me at induction."

"No limit on the generation of hot air," I add.

"Oscar knew I had to collaborate with the council on another youth project if I was to stand any chance of levering-in public funds for Ploughdown and he told me he had some promising material. I thought it might make an interesting piece of verbatim theatre. When I mentioned it to Councillor Evergreen, he begged me to go ahead. He saw it as a podcast on the council's website with award-winning potential. And he wanted it quickly, so there was no time to learn lines. We decided to use a technique called 'recorded delivery' instead."

"And what exactly is 'Verbatim Theatre'?" Geraldine asks, as though she's been passed a drink in a filthy glass.

"We use exactly the same words that people used at the event, so it's documentary style. But we cut up the order, bringing various strands together to make a story and build drama."

"You mean you edit." Geraldine writes on her notepad. "And who, exactly, edited the verbatim words of our councillors and these young people?"

"It was a collaborative effort," Josh says. "Me, Oscar, and some of his students. Councillor Evergreen insisted on authorising the final script. It's not like going through a text with a red pen. It's about spotting four or five ideas and selecting different passages to create a narrative."

"And this you can see is the bolt," I say. "The purpose of this is to open the breach, as you see. We can slide it rapidly backwards and forwards: we call this easing the spring."

Young Noah, unlike Geraldine, is warming to my contributions. He looks like he's ready for easing a bit of spring right now.

"Tell me about this narrative please, Josh. Briefly."

"We chose four topics: the withdrawal of vending machines so that students can only buy healthy snacks and drinks from the school canteen; the council's insistence on investing a chunk of its staff pension fund in tobacco companies; the…"

"And this makes theatre?"

"Like nothing you've seen or heard before. We feed the actors the real words through earpieces and they speak them aloud a second later with all the ums and errs, the throat clearing, the unfinished sentences. They don't interpret. They're like mediums channelling spirits and it has an uncanny effect. We have publicity-hungry councillors desperately wanting to seem with it, and idealistic students flush with their self-righteous certainties. And we're re-creating their exact mannerisms and meaning, but we've milked it for passion and humour and put a spotlight on it that makes it sound movingly truthful."

Geraldine says "Thank you, Josh," quickly, before I can get in with my line about japonica glistening like coral in all of the neighbouring gardens.

"So where did it go wrong?" she asks. She looks at Noah, who looks at Josh, who looks at me.

"Young people insisted on being young people," I say.

"And?"

"It turns out one of my lab techs has a crush on one of my lower sixths and thought it would be a gas to ask her for a date, live on stage, on opening night. He spliced a few extra words into one of his mate's feed: 'Bill says he thinks you're gorgeous and will you go to The Destroyers at the Town Hall with him next Friday?'"

Noah beams at the memory of it.

Geraldine scribbles to get it down verbatim.

"And because it's like he's on a moving staircase, because he's become like a medium channelling the spirit, his mate repeats perfectly, without thinking, 'Bill says he thinks you're gorgeous and will you go to The Destroyers at the Town Hall with him next Friday?'"

I repeat this on purpose, so Geraldine can report precisely. I want the exact words in her report because The Destroyers are a great band, and will get a kick out of a mention in dispatches. "But my lower sixths are well-practised in improvisation. Like mediums, come to think of it. So this one pulls her ear-piece out and says 'Speak for yourself, John.'"

"That's a reference to The Courtship of Miles Standish," Noah volunteers in a rush for Geraldine's benefit. "A poem by Longfellow about how a pilgrim from the Mayflower called Miles Standish courted the beautiful Priscilla Mullins using his friend John Alden as a go-between. I Googled it. But she really loved John, and after she said speak for yourself, he did, and eventually they married and…"

"Lived happily ever after. Thank you Noah," Geraldine says.

Josh explains that Ploughdown collaborated with Valeston Arts and Drama Department on adapting the Longfellow poem as a musical, last year.

"More to the point," I say, "Bill's mate, who is indeed called John, also has a deep, and now he discovers, requited crush on the said beauty in my lower sixth. He pulled out his ear-piece and spoke for himself. Graphically."

"Spare me that, please," Geraldine says. "Councillor Evergreen has shown me the newspaper cutting."

"It was just bad luck," Josh says, "that we cast this young John to play Councillor Evergreen. Councillor John Evergreen."

"Right," says Geraldine, snapping her notepad shut. "Let's take a comfort break. We'll reconvene for act two in five minutes."

"Yesterday we had daily cleaning," I say. "And tomorrow morning, we shall have what to do after firing. But today, today we have naming of parts."

VISION *by Gillian Dunstan*

The blindness crept up stealthily
as a fox in winter woods.
A jagged line blossomed, until
a brilliant jelly shivered, shimmered,
skated on the surface of my sight,
grew greedy,
devoured images, ate up the sense of words.

Fact: surgery.
Steely. Sharp as his knife
and I, all unprepared and cringing.

Two surgeons extracted jelly,
cut membrane, lasered holes,
inserted a gas bubble,
stitched me up.

Then I could only see a witch's ball
inside my head -
clearer than crystal, utterly opaque,
which, like a spirit level,
dipped and swayed with every breath.

Its perfect orb, outlined in deepest black,
fringed by fiery rings of red and gold,
held visions;
liquid shapes which morphed and melted
quicker than mountain clouds.
A fighter pilot (jet goggles and white scarf)
flowed into a fish with black forked tongue stuck out.
I jumped in fright. Already it was gone, as
many a motley clown leered at me from a tower.

That too became unhinged
by chains of dancing interwoven fractals
set in swirling mists, sea-green and violet
blue, shot through with dreamy pinks and mauves -
such vibrant depth of colour,
yet softer than a single flake of snow.

Sight was, of course, the prize.
But when my sight returned,
reality, too harsh and dull and flat,
lacking all that rich subtlety,
most disconcertingly,
failed to enchant.

TAKING CARE OF TOLLY *by Gerard Duffy*

I'm late and he's pissed off. I can see it in his face as I walk up to him. We stand in a long, wide corridor, big windows on one side throwing sunlight across the bored-looking villains draped over the benches waiting for their cases to be called.

"So?" says Tolly.

"Sorted." I look up at him. He towers over me. There's a lot of echoey clopping as the briefs hurry past in their cheap black suits, looking for their clients. Bizzies squeak about in their DM's, flicking through their notebooks, rehearsing their lines.

"Meaning?" His stare is all over me. He's wearing a new Armani and fresh trainers. His hair is gelled into stiff spikes - bit out of date, otherwise he could pass for a premier league footballer.

"We got to him. He's on message." He holds the stare on me another couple of seconds then relaxes, unwinding, growing even taller.

"Good lad, Jazz," he says, slapping my shoulder.

An usher in a gown comes over to us. Every Magistrates court I've ever been in seems to have an old boy like this one. They always look like they live in the cellar. This one's stooped and grey with a big snout.

"Name?" he says, his voice a throaty rasp.

"Adrian Toller," says Tolly.

The old boy licks his thumb, flicks through the stapled pages he's holding. "Number three, ten o'clock. What's yer previous?" Tolly rattles off his string. Old boy scribbles, casual. "Press're in, so comb yer hair and do yer flies up." He moves off to use the same line on someone else.

This is just the committal hearing. No big deal unless they remand you in custody. But they haven't the room. Even a murder charge is a walk-away unless the case against is a hundred percent and you're likely to leg it abroad.

"What did you do?" Now he's off the hook he can make a bit of chit-chat.

"Followed him to his access visit. Shat himself when he saw us sitting outside his ex's."

Tolly laughs his evil laugh. "D'you have a word?"

"A couple of well-chosens in his ear." We exchange smirks. "He saw the light."

He laughs again, slaps me on the shoulder again.

"I wouldn't've bovvered wiv the words. I'd've taken 'is face off." His grin fades. He's just reminded us why he's here today. He goes quiet, thinking about it. I can tell. I've known him since we were ten.

"Find out who she'd been fucking?" he says.

"Na. Never will now. You should've kicked it out of her before you popped her."

"I know." Regret in his voice. "I just lost it. Couldn't stop."

I see the lads coming in through the big plate glass doors, Ryan in the lead. He fancies himself in my shoes. They're loud, having a laugh. Their voices bounce off the high ceiling. Our crew's a presence. One you avoid if you've got any sense. They make to come over.

"Lads're here Toll." He doesn't even look round. He's got more distant lately. Hardly talks to them, lets me do all the running about. They keep asking what he's bringing to the party these days, apart from trouble. I give them a shake of my head to stop them coming then hold up three fingers. They obediently troop off to the court.

"Why'd she do it?" It's not a sad question. He isn't going to break down or anything. He's just puzzled. How anyone could cross him like that – with his reputation. I stare into space, like I don't get it either.

"Mr Toller!" Zuckie, Tolly's brief, breezes up. Born without a volume control. All hale and hearty. Tolly's a good customer. We all are. Got me off an Affray six months ago. We shake hands.

"Well, let's see now." He bustles, the way all lawyers do. Opens his file and looks through his papers. "CPS says strong circumstantial. Witness saw you leave the scene with alleged murder weapon. Records from your mobile phone company confirm time and place. Do we challenge or let it go to Crown?"

"Misunderstanding," says Tolly. "Witness has a different story now. Right Jazz?" They both look at me.

I nod. "Got his wires crossed."

Zuckie doesn't turn a hair. "So what does he say now?"

"He was trying to sell Tolly a gun. Tolly wasn't interested. End of. " I clock Tolly's face. He gives a little twist of his mouth and winks at me. He loves it.

"And he never saw Mr Toller holding a bloodied champagne bottle?" Zuckie arches his eyebrows like he's cross-examining me.

"No."

"I haven't seen a new statement."

"Only happened yesterday," I say.

Zuckie considers. "In that case we'll go for a Submission. Insufficient evidence. They should throw it out." He checks his watch. "In we go then."

He leads the way down the corridor, his leather shoes clicking along, our trainers silent. We're on display and we know it. Zuckie's suit is more expensive than most. Tolly and me – we're Faces. The lowlife check us out, but with sideways looks. Nobody wants to make the wrong kind of eye contact.

After Tolly's panicky phone call we all piled round to the flat. When we got there Tolly was still sitting in his car covered in blood for anyone to see, the bottle still in his hand. He was shaking. I'd never seen him like that before. I chucked a car blanket over him and one of the lads drove him off. Inside, everything was a mess, the room, with her – Sharon, his latest and greatest squeeze, lying twisted on the floor like a broken doll. He'd used the champagne bottle on her. There wasn't enough left of her face to recognise her. Vicious – you don't know what that word means till you've met Tolly. Her hair was the same, and I knew the green dress. We got down to business. Two of the lads wrapped her in a blanket, took her out and stuck her in the boot of my motor. Ryan took my keys and drove them all out to Essex to dig a hole for her. I stayed to torch the flat – kill the DNA. Before I did, I walked around the living room looking at the blood on the walls, over the carpet. Then I went into the bedroom. It was as neat and tidy as always – untouched. I knelt by the bed, ran my hand under the duvet and over the cotton sheet, feeling its familiar touch. I bent down and put my head on the pillow, let it rest there for a minute, breathing in her scent for the last time and trying not to cry.

We stroll into court three, Tolly looking cocky. The place is all fake wood and comfy seats these days. Tolly and Zuckie head for the desks at the front. It's busier than usual, nearly full. There are several scribblers, more than just local – right up Tolly's street. He wants to be a celebrity crim, the new Kenny Noye or John Bindon. The lads have saved me a seat in the middle of them. I slide in and take my place. The usher settles everyone down and we get started. The clerk pops up and reads the charge sheet. Then it's time to hear from the prosecution. A bald guy from the CPS gets up and starts explaining that his witness has bottled out. Tolly looks round and grins at us. The Muppet looks at Zuckie.

"What is the Defense's response?"

Zuckie rises to his feet slowly, making the most of his moment. "We submit that in the circumstances there is insufficient evidence to proceed and that case be dismissed."

The Muppet looks back at Baldy.

"We have an alternative witness," Baldy says, dome glistening. Tolly's jaw almost drops off his face. Zuckie goes red.

"We haven't been informed," he bleats.

"Materialised only this morning, I'm afraid," says Baldy. "There wasn't time to inform you." He turns back to the Muppet. "May I call him?"

"Proceed."

Baldy turns and looks at me. I rise and make my way past the lads. Ryan looks up and gives me a wink. I wink back.

WAKING *by Sue Belfrage*

To lie on the lip of an eye,
Slide the dip of its thin rim,
Then prise; let shards of prisms in,
Refracting white.

Deep deep, round bubbles of knowing rise,
Catch under a surface of skin,
Pushing to break, to open wide,
Tracking the long weight of limbs.

The body, a diver's suit with heavy feet,
This head, a helmet of bone.
Ah – to sink back down to the warmth,
Adrift in the dreaming pool.

The Yeovil Literary Prize

2012 Commended

Chip Tolson *Everyone is Talking About It*	59
Hilary Davies *Examination*	64
Ruth Driscoll *For Gracie*	65
Sharon Keating *Chanticleer's Egg*	69
Carol Lovejoy Edwards *The Glass Fish*	70
Roger Iredale *I-Raq*	74
Suzanne Furness *From Byron to Shelley*	75
Blanche Sears *Negative Equity*	79
J A Brooks *More Than a Butterfly*	80
Sharon Black *On the Line*	85
Karla Dearsley *Blind Alleys*	86
Sharon Keating *Shrink*	90
Michael Roe *An Equation for Justice*	91

EVERYONE IS TALKING ABOUT IT
by Chip Tolson

She'd been told there would be a three-month probationary period; still a long way to go it being only the third Monday meeting Amanda Chater had chaired. Monday Reviews were a routine as old as the department store itself. Sharp at 10 o'clock on the first morning of every working week the Heads of Section gathered in the boardroom to run through a standing agenda of topics. They had gone easy on Amanda for the past two weeks; she knew it wouldn't last. You don't get promoted over the heads of long serving staff members and not pick up resentment along the way.

'The bootleg trousers, the ones made in China, we've had constant complaint about the seam stitching,' Mrs Prichard was speaking. Amanda had started work at the department store five years before as a junior in Maggie Prichard's section. Maggie had been twenty years at Meadows working her way up to be a Section Head.

Meadows hadn't been Amanda's first choice of career; she'd planned to be a lawyer; you need a law degree for that and she'd missed the chance of getting to university. Still she had got her Business Studies Diploma at college, moved a hundred miles from home to find employment and Meadows were good employers. Now she was making her mark.

Amanda knew there had been gossip, a nod and a wink between the Section Heads implying her promotion was prompted by the General Manager's roving eye. That was unfair. She got on well with 'Mr Frank', he was certainly good looking and a bachelor, but it was hard work that had won her promotion and she was determined to show she was chosen on merit.

'Has the problem been taken up with the Buyers?'

'We should never have gone to the Far East, we should have stayed with the British factories we know.' Mrs Prichard looked at the nodding heads round the table. 'They wouldn't allow poor seam stitching out of the factory.'

'But at a price; we have to compete. It's the economics of the market place.'

'It's shoddy cost-cutting, if you ask me.' Mrs Prichard was determined to have her say and Amanda knew it was true. The China orders had been hastily put in place to catch a fashion surge.

'It's economics and a matter of quality control,' she insisted looking

Maggie in the eye yet sensing the meeting was against her. 'There is no reason why these Far East goods should be below standard. We have to ensure proper quality control at the factories.'

Without any warning the boardroom door burst open. Charlie Potts looked round the room. There was something amiss he was not his usual smart security presence.

'Sorry, is Mr Frank in?' Sgt Potts, for many years a soldier, now the morning shift Security Supervisor, was flustered.

'He's away Charlie. He won't be back until tomorrow,' Amanda told him. Was she imagining the glimmer of resentment on Mrs Prichard's face? No one had told Maggie that Frank Meadows, the third generation to own and manage Meadows Department Store, had gone away. 'Is there a problem on the floor, Charlie?'

'Big time, Miss Chater.'

'What is it?'

'We've pulled a shoplifter, a posh lady; she's kicking up a fuss; says she's Lady something and a friend of the Chief Constable.'

'And was she shoplifting?'

'Yes, got her positive on the CCTV more than once, woollens and costume jewellery.'

'Well?'

'There's nothing on her, clean as a whistle, she must have dumped it.'

'Can you give her a warning?'

'Says she's going to sue us; can you come and have a word with her, Miss Chater.'

One by one faces round the table turned to Amanda. It wouldn't wait. 'Yes, I'll come. Mrs Prichard, will you take over the meeting. I may be a while.'

Maggie Prichard took heart from her preferment over the other Heads of Section. 'I will, Miss Chater.'

In her office Amanda checked herself in the mirror, pursing her lips, confident she had been right to colour her hair auburn and pleased she had chosen her dark pinstripe suit to start the week. She decided to put on her gold frame Gucci glasses to look older.

Sgt Potts worked the controls of Amanda's monitor in the corner of the room, bringing up two sections from the security tape. The woman was seen in both confident and skilled. In a flash a sweater and scarf disappeared inside her coat.

'She's done that before,' Amanda ran the tape back and watched the woman again.

'She's a professional if you ask me,' agreed Charlie. 'That's why she ditched the stuff before we got to her.'

'And nothing has been found in any of the usual places?'

'Nothing, but they're still searching.'

'Let's go.' Amanda didn't enjoy confrontation yet it went with the territory. Frank Meadows would use his charm in this situation; she had to do it her way. She gave a thin smile to Sgt Potts as they got out of the lift on the ground floor and made their way through to the back office.

The interview room was stark; a plain table with four upright chairs, a microphone and tape recorder. There had been a bottle of water and glasses until a recent accused had grabbed the bottle and struck out at Sgt Potts.

The woman was seated, heavily made up and Amanda guessed wearing a wig. Her coat had once been expensive, but might have been found in any charity shop. Ignoring the woman's disdain Amanda introduced herself as the Deputy General Manager of the store.

'And do you know who I am?'

'Sgt Potts has told me you are Lady Butler-Perkins, Madam.'

'And my husband is a well respected member of the House of Lords.'

'That may be, Madam; we have reason to believe you took goods from this store intending not to pay for them.'

'Don't be ridiculous, how dare you make such accusations, you stupid woman.'

'You were recorded on camera, Madam. A sweater, a scarf and some costume jewellery.' There was no way this woman was going to let slip any hint of guilt. Without the goods being found on her, even with the CCTV tape evidence, there was little chance of obtaining a conviction. She needed to find a way of ending the interview in the store's favour.

A knock on the door and a folded note was handed to Sgt Potts; he looked at it briefly before passing it to Amanda. The single word "nothing" was written on the paper.

'I'm going to sue your tin-pot store for punitive damages. You see if I don't. I'll bankrupt you.'

There was a familiarity about this woman, not of her dress or her style, but something about her face. Had Amanda seen her in the store on another day, perhaps her picture in the local paper opening a fete with her Lordly husband at her side? They were going to have to let her go. Amanda was not concerned at the woman's boast of friendship with the Chief Constable, an old chestnut. She feared there would be mutterings on the shop floor that the incident had been poorly handled; it wasn't the crisis she wanted Frank Meadows to come back to, not after the Directors had put their trust in her to run the business in the General Manager's absence.

The woman took out a packet of cigarettes, fiddling with her lighter, flipping it over in her hand.

Amanda remembered.

'This is a no smoking area, Madam.'

'Your Ladyship, if you don't mind,' came the belligerent rejoinder.

'Oh, come on, cut the crap. You are no more a lady than I am.'

The woman sat opened mouthed a cigarette halfway to her mouth. Sgt Potts stared at Amanda. For a moment the small room was hushed, just the hum of the tape recorder. Amanda's stomach churned.

'How dare you, impudent woman. I'll see that you lose your job for this.'

'Beacon Street Comprehensive, Snaresborough: 1993.' The shot struck home; the woman couldn't speak for a moment; Sgt Potts eased into his chair. Amanda stared across the table as the woman hesitated to meet her eye.

'I have no idea what you mean,' her eyes were downcast.

'I think you do. The sixth form, Set B.'

'You're talking gibberish, woman. I wish to leave and you will be hearing from my solicitor.'

'You will not be leaving until you have signed an undertaking never to visit this store again. And we will be reporting this matter to the police.'

'This is outrageous. I wish to leave.' The woman pushed back her chair. Sgt Potts strode across to the door to bar the woman's way.

'I wish to telephone my husband, Lord Butler-Perkins. Get me a telephone.' The woman was shouting.

'Do you recall the matter of the crib sheet found under a desk after the mathematics exam?'

The woman's face reddened, beads of sweat broke out on her upper lip. 'Who are you?'

'I told you when we first met. I am the Deputy General Manager of this department store. It was not just that one senior schoolgirl had been cheating in the exam; what mattered was that the cheat put the blame onto a younger girl in her set.'

'This has nothing to do with me. I demand that you let me pass. I am leaving.'

'Mary Richards, you don't know when to stop digging do you. I know who you are, I know what you did, and the girl you framed is well known to me. You are not Lady anyone, you are a habitual shoplifter and I expect, if we review past CCTV tapes, we will see that you have been shoplifting in this store on previous occasions.'

A broad smile crossed Sgt Potts face as a strained intake of breath preceded the woman's tears. 'I'm desperate. It's true I'm not Lady anybody and my pathetic husband has deserted me.'

'Sgt Potts, you can deal with the formalities. Please ensure that Ms Richards signs the usual undertaking and that all store detectives are given her description. I have business to attend upstairs.' Amanda stood up and turned to the woman 'Mary, let this be a warning to you. What you have done today is wrong whatever your motivation; what you did at the time of those examinations was despicable. The young schoolgirl you framed lost her opportunity to take her exams that summer and didn't get to university.'

'It's just my rotten luck to come all this way from Snaresborough to get sussed by a hometown girl. Look in the Lloyd Loom laundry baskets if you want to find your wretched goods,' she said with a resigned air. Amanda threw a questioning glance at Charlie Potts. Surely someone had looked in the laundry baskets?

Amanda sat behind her desk with her eyes closed, willing the turmoil she felt inside to settle. Many times she had tried to forget that summer of disappointment. Now for the first time she felt she had exorcised the ghost. There was a knock at her door; it was Maggie Prichard.

'Amanda, I've been on to the Buyers and given them a roasting on the China products. They admit they didn't put proper quality control in place. Oh, and well done with the shoplifter. Everyone is talking about it.'

EXAMINATION *by Hilary Davies*

'Look directly into my eyes
And tell me, as I pass my right hand
In an arc around you, when it disappears':
My gaze is clean and dispassionate as a lazer
Into the window of this stranger's brain.
Though we mimic the trajectory of lovers,
Yet we find nothing but capillaries and mucus
In each other ; I reflect how his eye
Is only a distension of water.
'Now I want you to touch, very lightly,
My palm several times: first eyes open'
--His hands are slats of rubber—'then closed'.
Your skin was silk, its coolness made me swoon.
How the tapered fingers traced my arteries
In the slow afternoons, the subcutaneous electricals
Flashing from finger tip to tip!
'Relax your arm on mine a moment'; I'm limp
As a rag doll now, but do you remember
How you led me a fandango of longing
Hip to hip? 'This time, without looking,
I want you to tell me each time I touch you':
O for the mornings of such exhortations unnecessary,
When we passed muster at that guessing game.
Now my repeated 'Yes' echoing in the operations room
Leaps the heads of these students, their fumbling gestures,
Snaps back the rhythms with which we held each other
In that sweet, mutual dance of desire.

FOR GRACIE *by Ruth Driscoll*

Sunday

It's the night before Gracie's first day at school. Think I have got everything sorted.

Warm winter coat
3 x green jumper
3 x grey dress
3 x white shirts
2 x tie (elastic not real)
Ankle socks, long socks
PE kit (shorts, joggers, T shirt, plimsolls)
Pack all this inside green drawstring bag.

She's so excited. Been trying everything on all week. I've washed and ironed everything and folded it nicely. Just checked on her and she looked small. Black curls stuck to her forehead, cheeks all pink with sweat, little arms and legs curled up around her teddy. She'll be fine. I've been here before.

Monday

First day. She slept late and I didn't want to wake her. Got dressed and ready on time, though. Her dad went to work late so we could take photos in the garden.

Grace in uniform – jumper on
Grace in uniform – jumper off
Grace in coat against hedge + daddy
Grace + daddy by front door
Grace + daddy in front of gate
Grace + you (if you want)
Keep the light behind you at all times.

I'll put the best one in a frame for the house and send the others to Grandma. Gracie talked all the way about how she is going to be the cleverest in class, get stars for being good, gobble up her dinner like a doggy. Then we reached the classroom door. Hugged me tight like she was never going to let go. When the teacher stuck her head out, Gracie lay on the floor, kicked her legs, and screamed her bloody head off. Teacher pulled her inside and shut the door.

Tuesday

Gracie a bit happier today. Hugged me round my chest instead of my neck. Bit of screeching but no kicking thank god. Teacher didn't have to pull so hard to get her inside. Mind felt foggy on the walk home. Focused hard on the list.

Sort out baby toys and clothes
Take to charity shop
Wash and iron sheets (Grace)
Pack suitcases (you)
Ring Roy to organise van (in the afternoon - he works nights).

Mind still a bit foggy in the afternoon. She's got so many clothes the bloody cupboard is collapsing. Too many toys as well. That girl'd be spoiled rotten if I hadn't taught her to say please and thank you and eat her banana with a fork not her fingers. Teacher said she cried for me today when she was dressing up, in the home corner, at circle time, and in the dinner hall. Head cleared when I scooped up Gracie. Shut the classroom door behind us. Sun harsh on our heads.

Wednesday

Gracie kissed me with just two tears today. Then tore off with the teacher. She told me don't forget to bring her Jammy Dodgers when I pick her up, but I couldn't find Jammy Dodgers in any of the shops next to the

Dry-cleaners
Post Office
Chemist and
Supermarket.

Drizzling after dinner. Went all the way to West Dulwich but still couldn't find the damn Jammie Dodgers. I know Gracie likes marshmallows too so bought a big soft packet and tucked it in my coat to keep warm. Her Dad called to say he was coming home early so he'd go and get Gracie. Damn drizzle all day's done my head no good at all. Drums on the double-glazed door. Stops me sleeping.

Thursday

Gracie told me to go this morning cos no grown ups are allowed at school. She said,
　Look!
　You're the only grown up in this classroom!!
　YOU GO!!!
　She is now an independent woman. Made me feel so proud. Thought my chest would burst open with it. Clouds burst open when I walked home.

My list is short now:

Unassemble bed and pack flat
Pack suitcases (if haven't already)
Hoover and dust room (use Pledge, don't dry dust).

Finished work early today. Hoover was giving me one big headache. Think it could be hay fever but it's the wrong time of year. Maybe it's a migraine? I didn't sleep last night or the night before. Gracie so happy at pick up.

Friday

Gracie's mum said she was taking Gracie today so she knows how to do it. She wanted to hold Gracie's hand. Gracie wanted to hold mine. Gracie's cheek was on mine and our hair got all mixed up. She smelt sour like a cold, smeared snot on my shoulder, buried her head in my stomach. Then we reached the classroom door. She hugged me tight like she was never going to let go. Gracie's mum pushed her inside and shut the door. I asked if she wanted to see Gracie playing dressing up, in the home corner, at circle time or in the dinner hall. But she had to rush.

Saturday

It is snowing. Didn't want to do

Weekend food shop
Spring clean whole house (if you have time!)

today. I'm so knackered. I've barely slept a wink all week. Had to lie down after lunch with a wet flannel on my head because I've got a temperature coming too. This is definitely a migraine and I'm going to make an appointment to see the doctor about it. It's there from the moment I wake and it is killing me. Caught the bus to the big Sainsbury's on the hill in the afternoon and asked the Customer Services lady. She found me the last packet of Jammie Dodgers at the back of the shelf. Gracie was so chuffed she nearly knocked me over.

Saturday

I asked Gracie's mum and dad if they are going to tell Gracie, or if they want me to do it. They said they will tell her after I've gone. Roy came with the van in the sleet. We got soaked loading up. Gracie asked if I was going on holiday when she saw the suitcases. Her mum said yes. Gracie smelt sour like a cold, smeared snot on my shoulder, buried her head in my stomach. Hugged her tight like I was never going to let go. It's ok. I've been here before.

CHANTICLEER'S EGG *by Sharon Keating*

Ice sculpture's too cool to crow the day.
A plume of tail feathers, glass blades
gesturing at the snow, weathering
the temperature, drip by drip,
quick, quick. Slow.
One astonished antler!
Brilliantine crown, brittle rubber fingers
in perpendicular surprise, coxcombing
the crest with an undulating frown.
Transfixed in ice, riveted mid-croak,
crystallising that moment before the fox
has you by the throat. Its alchemy.
The alchemy of birds in flight,
bodies rising up heavier than air.
And rare, the compacted solidity of ice
aloft in its own element, carvable
as marble, quarrying a swirl
of aerial feathers cloven from fluidity,
now frozen. Ice daggers drawn
now folded, all sharp edges
moulded into shapes of movement -
rope muscles, tadpoles, fat pears falling.
Icicles trickle and thaw undoing the spell,
returning the rooster backwards
to bits of broken coracle -
relics, razor-bills, scalloped frills.
Vanishing in a cockatrice. A glare-
eyed clutch; cracked cockle shell.

THE GLASS FISH *by Carol Lovejoy Edwards*

Rosie Lloyd met Amber McKie outside the main entrance to the Swan at Gamston. Today Amber's shoulder length hair was crimson red and her eyes green. She wore a pink tie-died T-shirt and a full length purple skirt. Her bag was knitted from odds and ends of wool in all shades of the rainbow and misshapen with use.

"Hello Rosie. It's nice to finally meet you in person." Amber leaned in to give Rosie a hug, like long lost friends.

"Good to see you too. Let's go grab a table." Rosie led the way inside her many bangles rhythmically accompanying them. Rosie's long black skirt almost covered the laces on her doc marten boots. The tassels brushed the floor as she walked and Amber marvelled at how she never managed to tread on one. Her bright yellow T-shirt matched Rosie's personality. The red flowers and ribbons in her hair clashed with its natural carrot shade. Her fingers held costume jewellery of various shapes and sizes, large flower rings, a small fish shaped one and one on her little finger that resembled a charm bracelet.

Amber (aka Amanda Smart, aka Julia Stewart and Teresa Galton) followed her new friend into the warmth. The pub was busy and there were only a few tables left. They chose to sit next to the window with a group of pensioners to their other side all talking at once. The talking stopped abruptly as the pensioners all stared at the two women, the interlopers. The weekly outing of the Whatton Lunch Club wasn't used to such colour. The two men, Roy and Bill, stared open mouthed all social niceties forgotten. Eileen and Barbara, hair done especially that morning, smiled at the new comers checked them out and went back to bitching about the bingo club. Their unwritten code wouldn't allow them to discuss the brightly coloured women until they got home. Or to the car at least.

"Hello," chirped Rosie. That cheerfulness had come through forcefully on Rosie's Facebook page leading Amber to hope for a short lunch. It was irritating in cyber space. She imagined the real thing would be more intense.

Having given their order to the waitress, Rose peppered Amber with questions. "I don't know much about Amber McKie. Your Facebook profile doesn't reveal much about you." She smiled at Amber inviting her to divulge.

I don't know much about her either, thought Amber. *Here goes.* "I was born in Leicestershire, moved to London in my 20s and then to Nottingham when I got married. That's it."

Rosie asked a few questions about Amber's husband her work and her family. The answers were short: Martin, craft stall on the market and none. Shrugging, Rosie shared every detail of her life, husband and children with Amber. Amber sincerely hoped there wouldn't be a quiz later as she tuned out and looked around her.

Rosie kept up the chatter all during the first course whilst Amber made the appropriate noises from time to time. Amber couldn't get to the main fast enough. Rosie gushed over the food as the waitress placed sausage and mash down in front of her and a plate of fish and chips in front of Amber. As usual for these kinds of places the plates were twice the size of any you had at home and jammed full of food. Amber's battered cod took up most of the plate and was artfully laid down the centre with garden peas on one side and homemade chips on the other. Rosie's onion topped sausages rested on a mound of creamy mashed potatoes surrounded by a moat of gravy.

Tucking into their meals finally slowed down the rate at which Rosie could chatter. "This is delicious," said Amber through a mouthful of chips and chewed cod. Rosie looked up from her food mild disgust evident at the sight of Amber's open mouth with half masticated food. Amber suddenly closed her eyes and put her hand over her mouth and nose. She gently sneezed whilst scrabbling in her voluminous bag for a tissue. Having found what she was looking for and holding it very carefully she manoeuvred the tissue over her mouth. She sneezed again into the tissue this time, trying to retain as much of her food as possible.

Once her sneezing had subsided she returned the tissue to her bag. Mission accomplished. "Sorry about that," said Amber. "Must be some dust flying around somewhere."

"Amber, you're bleeding."

Amber grabbed another tissue from her bag and unfolded it dabbing her nose.

"Not your nose it's your mouth."

"Oh," cried a now distressed Amber. She dabbed at her mouth and emptied the remains of her food into the tissue. She laid the crumpled item on the table and examined its contents. There was definitely blood and also a few tiny specks of glass sparkled back at her. She smiled and folded the tissue leaving it on the table. The pensioners at the next table looked over in disgust.

"Get a waitress barked Rosie to the pensioners. "She's bleeding" Bill shuffled off at his own top speed. Rosie got out of her seat and put her arm around Amber.

"You're still bleeding. Let me have a look in your mouth."

Reluctantly, although cheering inside, Amber opened her mouth.

Rosie stuck her finger in and pulled out a slither of glass no bigger than a hair. "Oh my God. You've eaten glass."

The young fair haired waitress appeared at their table and Rosie exclaimed, "There's glass in her food."

"I'll get the manager." The waitress scurried off in panic mode. She burst into the manager's office startling both of them and managed to gabble out that someone was bleeding from eating glass.

"Bring her here right away."

Back at the table the waitress was still heavily flustered. Everyone was looking at them from the surrounding tables. Why did this have to happen on her first day and at such a busy time? She needed this job and didn't want to get fired. "I'll take you to the manager's office. Follow me."

Amber couldn't believe how well this one was going. Rosie had been a perfect pick doing all the fussing and complaining for her.

"Bring that plate of food," Rosie barked at the quivering wreck of a waitress. "I want the manager to see it. There's more glass in that fish." The tables all around echoed the sound of cutlery being replaced on tables and dishes being pushed away from diners. As they walked to the manager's office other diners stared at the spots of blood on Amber's lips and chin. "Glass in her food." Was heard several times as they wove through the tables. It seemed like the whole restaurant knew before they reached the manager's office. Amber was really pleased. They were ushered into the modern room with its IKEA desk and chairs. The manager was in his forties with a receding hairline and a slight weight problem. Rosie took over as they were shown in to the office. Amber settled herself in the visitors chair feet barely reaching the floor.

"There's glass in your fish. Its cut her mouth. I think she's still bleeding. You'd better call an ambulance."

"I have done. It's on its way. Have a seat and tell me what's happened." He directed Rosie to a chair and looked expectantly at Amber. She started to answer him when Rosie interrupted. Again.

"You know what's happened. Here." She snatched the plate from the waitress and shoved it at the manager. "Glass in Fish." Rose talked slowly and loudly to the manager as she did to all foreigners.

"Tissue," Amber touched Rosie on the shoulder who produced fresh supplies for her. Amber dropped the blood stained tissue onto the manager's desk. He then used a rule to flick it into the bin.

"So what are you going to do about it?" Rosie questioned the manager.

"The ambulance is on its way."

"It's not just about that. What about compensation for my injuries discomfort and emotional distress?"

"She's got a point you know. She's been ever so upset."

Amber congratulated herself on her choice of Rosie. This was going much better than expected. Rosie's indignation could only add pounds to Amber's financial gain. "My mouth is really sore, Rosie. My throat feels itchy." On cue Amber coughed more blood into yet another tissue.

"Well I have a contact at the Nottingham Post who would be delighted with this story. Big chain like this one. It could even go national. Is that what you want?"

The manager glared at Rosie but didn't have time to formulate an answer as the paramedics arrived. They entered the manager's office and began their questions.

"What happened?"

"I sneezed," said Amber "I had a mouthful of food at the time and there was glass in it."

"She's cut her mouth quite badly inside," added Rosie.

"Let's have a look."

Amber opened her mouth wide and the paramedic shone a miniature torch into the cavity. "There's still some glass embedded into your cheeks so I'll get that out now." His partner passed him tweezers and held the torch for him as he slowly removed several slivers. Amber cried out in pain once or twice as the paramedics worked.

"We'll need to take you to A and E because there may be small pieces left that I can't see."

"You'd better get your cheque book out," Amber said to the manager. Rosie said, "I'm sorry love. I can't come to the hospital as I have to go and pick up my kids. Will you be OK?"

"Just fine. Don't worry. You've been great Rosie. A really good friend. Thanks for all your help."

Rosie waved as Amber was safely installed in the ambulance and the doors closed. As Amber lay back on the stretcher she opened the piece of paper the manager had slipped into her hand as she left. "£5,000," was all it said.

Amber smiled to herself. A good day's work. She felt in her bag for the other tissue containing glass. She always carried a spare, just in case.

In the car park Rosie was talking to the manager, Detective Sergeant Case. "I think we've got her this time."

"Well done DC Edwards. Now get down to A and E and arrest her before she has a chance to get rid of the evidence in her bag."

I-RAQ *by Roger Iredale*

I am the face that flickered briefly on your TV
late one night when missiles shouted hallelujahs
over blacked-out buildings, and the sky
collapsed in debris, and bridges cracked
their spines, and the lights went out for good.

I was the startled eyeballs staring into camera
as your zombies flailing flashlights kicked
my door down, demanding sons who know
no answers to no questions, and did not
stumble back to tell the tale. And never will.

You glimpsed me later, dodging tanks that crushed
foundations, walls, rooftiles meticulously
into dust so fine the land forgot it once
embraced a home where parents planted
seeds of happiness, and good fortunes grew.

But you missed the children finding yellow toys
that vanished in a puff of smoke, or breathing
old uranium out of dust you sent us
in carcasses of metal left as monuments
to liberty and freedom from the barrel of a gun.

We are the hollow men, the vacant women,
empty children. We are your breakfast news,
backdrop to your hogroast, ogres of your sleep.
We live in forests of dishonour, deserts
of disdain. You do not know us for yourselves.

FROM BYRON TO SHELLEY *by Suzanne Furness*

I watch her. Bent over, toiling away at the hard earth. Thick hair caught back from her face with a mother of pearl slide. It was her crowning glory when she was younger, pale gold with a soft wave. All the boys wanted to run their fingers through it and all the girls eyed it jealously. It is still a similar colour, although now it needs the added assistance of a trip to the hairdresser to eliminate the dull greys that keep appearing.

She sits back on her heels and stretches her back – *Julia. My Julia.*

I felt such pride the day she agreed to be my wife. Twenty eight years of happy marriage and two sons, I'd so much to be thankful for.

I recall the day we met so vividly. Early May 1979, Margaret Thatcher had just been elected as Prime Minister and people buzzed with talk of the future. It was a warm day, the air tinged with the anticipation of summer. The park scattered with a carpet of cherry blossom, the few flowers that remained on the trees danced in the breeze like tutu clad ballerinas.

She sat beneath one of these trees, her back leaning against the trunk, legs curled to one side, reading a book that lay in front of her. Her free hand absently plucked at tufts of grass.

Instantly my heart jumped. It was as if my life till now had been incomplete, a journey to this moment. Involuntarily, I stopped, pulling Byron's lead just a little too hard. He yelped in response, causing her to look up from her book.

She smiled. I blushed - caught in the depths of her blue green eyes.

"Hi," she said softly, "Lovely dog," she added, nodding at Byron.

"Th-Thanks," I stammered, "He's a golden retriever," I said needlessly.

"I know," she said, with the hint of a laugh. "My grandparents used to have one."

All background noise faded to the merest whisper as she stood up. She wore a lightly gathered, floral top that sat just on her shoulders and a pair of brown, wide legged trousers that almost covered her platform shoes.

I could not speak, yet my head was suddenly filled with the words of one of my favourite poems; *There be none of Beauty's daughters With a magic like Thee.*

"What's his name?" Standing so close, the scent of roses filled my nostrils as she reached down to rub the dog's ears.

"Byron," I managed, with a little cough. At the sound of his name the dog licked my hand and banged my leg with his wagging tail. He loved attention.

"Oh, like the poet?" The beauty giggled as Byron turned to lick her hand too.

"Yes, I'm rather fond of poetry." Would she think me foolish?

"Oh me too," she enthused, and I felt myself relax under her warm smile. "I was just reading some as it happens." She pointed to her book that still lay fluttering on the ground.

"My name's Julia," she held out her hand and I relished in the softness of her skin. Could she feel the electricity tingling down my arm at her touch?

"William. Pleased to meet you, Julia." For the briefest of moments our eyes locked. I was gripped by the overwhelming fear that Julia may vanish, our paths never crossing again.

"Would you care to take a walk with Byron and me?" I asked, bravely.

"I'd love to, thanks." Julia scooped her book into a cloth bag and slung it casually over her shoulder.

We walked in silence for a few minutes, but strangely it wasn't an awkward silence, more one of mutual companionship where words aren't always necessary.

I let Byron off his lead for a run. We watched him race excitedly from tree to tree, nose surfing the ground, searching for the most interesting smells. We laughed as he bounded after a glossy red setter that he knew well. The young couple who owned the setter called over, "Think our Bonnie's in love with your Byron, she's a right flirt!"

By the time Byron finally returned from his games, panting loudly but still with enough energy to wag his tail furiously, I'd learnt that Julia was in her last year at the local arts college studying illustration. She planned to travel around Europe over the summer and then start looking for a job in the Autumn.

"My dream is to illustrate children's books," she told me, eyes alight with excitement at the prospect.

I was a few years older than Julia and already teaching English at the comprehensive school in the next town. "My dream is to show 8E the joy of poetry!" I laughed, "I'm sure your dreams are much more realistic though!"

We walked slowly to the edge of the park, both of us reluctant for the meeting to end. Finally, reaching the metal railings, the fear bubbled to the surface again. "I don't suppose you fancy getting a cuppa do you, there's a little place just down the road, where I sometimes go. It has outside tables so we can take Byron ..." I realised I was gabbling, but I couldn't stop, thankfully she cut in.

"Sounds great, I could do with a cup of Earl Grey."

Over cups of tea and buttery scones with strawberry jam, we chatted easily. It was clear we shared so many interests, not just a love of poetry. Afterwards, as we strolled back down the road towards her shared flat, it seemed the most natural thing in the world for Julia to slip her arm through mine. And, by the time we reached her red front door with the peeling paint, we had already arranged to meet for dinner later that evening, at a little restaurant by the river.

I travelled to Europe with her over the summer, it had been the most wonderful time and we hadn't wanted it to end. But as September beckoned we returned to England; me to my teaching job and Julia to her job applications.

A week before Christmas that year Julia moved into my little two bedroom terraced house and we were a proper family – me, Julia and Bryon.

She found a job with a small independent book publisher and we started to save for the future.

Three years later we married at a beautiful old church in the village where Julia's parents lived. Byron was there, as always. Julia bought him a smart bow tie to strap to his collar for the day. He'd loved all the attention.

But all that had been a lifetime ago...

Julia has nearly finished her work. A pretty red rose bush bobs in the breeze. Slipping off the soil encrusted, gardening gloves she puts them into a plastic bag, along with her trowel. As she stands she pulls a tissue from her pocket and blows her nose.

Suddenly she spins round; eyes dart about as though searching for something. I notice her blue green eyes look misty and the dark rings under them are new.

I should go to her, comfort her... she smiles and I ache for her, it seems almost physical and I rush closer, O*h Julia*.

Then stop. Trembling. A figure approaches. Tall and handsome, his gold hair flops in front of his face as he puts a comforting arm around Julia's shoulders and she leans gratefully into him.

"That looks lovely, Mum," he says gently. "Dad would have approved."

"Thank you darling," Julia smiles at her son, *our* son, as she hastily pushes another tear from her cheek. "I think he would too."

Here lies William Grayson (1955 – 2010)

Beloved husband and loving father
Yet did I love thee to the last
As fervently as thou

"Dad always loved Byron," Matthew said, laying a kiss on his mother's head.

What I would not have given at that moment to hold my Julia one last time. I think that until now I hadn't believed it impossible. Surely not even death could separate us. I call out, *Julia*, and for a fraction of a second, hope soars as my love turns and looks straight at me. But then the moment has gone and she bends to retrieve the plastic bag.

"Come on Matthew, Tom will be wondering where we've got to." Julia slips her free hand through her eldest son's arm and they turn and walk away from me. I follow, unwilling to give in, yet.

They are chatting, mother and son. "I told Thomas we would be home by four; he's bringing his new girlfriend for dinner this evening."

"Young love, eh!" Matthew laughs, opening the car boot and taking the bag from his mother.

A beautiful golden retriever puppy bounces up and down excitedly in the back seat. Something else that's new.

"Okay, Okay, calm down Shelley!" Matthew grabs the exuberant dog's collar to stop her leaping out of the open door.

And then I do finally realise it's time to let go. My family needs to move on. *Julia, I love you,* I whisper, *I always will. Goodbye my love.*

Julia, car door in hand, stops and turns towards me again.

"What's the matter, Mum?" Matthew slams the boot. "You look a little pale."

"What, oh no, really I'm fine, Matthew. I just... for a moment I..." Julia shakes her head. "It's just my mind playing tricks, it's been a funny sort of day – finally seeing Dad's headstone in place, my mind's playing tricks on me."

"Come on, let's go, I could do with a cup of tea." Julia gets into the passenger seat and shuts the door. But her eyes never leave the spot where I am. I see her lips move and I somehow know exactly what she has just said, and I wonder whether she truly believes it. "What kind of a fool believes in ghosts?"

NEGATIVE EQUITY *by Blanche Sears*

The agents' letters clamp upon the mat.
White leaves, lacking the depth of Autumn's colour,
Flutter persistently but hopefully into my life,
The relics of another's cast-off dreams.
Houses rife with ring mains and panes of double glass,
New bathrooms fully-tiled, deep freezers packed
All pass in euphemistic phrases to beguile the soul.
Patios, verandahs, houses of character requiring
Modernisation, gentrification, sterilisation,
They pluck the pennies from unwilling hands.
Deposits paid, contracts exchanged, bank loans secured,
We join the many millions, mortgaged-racked,
Heedless as Faust. The Mephistophelian agent smiles,
Pockets his fee; while we, vacantly possessed,
Shut fast our doors on life. And in the shadows, silently,
The Debt Collector waits.

MORE THAN A BUTTERFLY *by J A Brooks*

I was in the garden when the letter arrived. Being one of those perfect summer days, a breeze pleasantly cooled the skin, and soft cotton wool clouds floated in a clear blue sky. So where else would I be on such a day?

Having gathered the post I sat in the shade. Recognising her letter in its usual red envelope it was the first to be opened. It started as usual with "my dearest friend" and as always finished with a beautiful drawing of a butterfly, having become her signature many years ago; first as a little squiggle with wings, and with time emerging into many exquisite specimens. This one proved her very best; so real that as I unfolded the page, it fluttered. First startled, I quickly realized a butterfly had landed upon the page, imitating her drawing perfectly. I sat in awe as I witnessed nature complimenting Hoshi's creation. As the butterfly fluttered away I wanted to tell her immediately of this amazing phenomena; I went into the house to phone Hoshi in Japan. I picked up the phone, but then, slowly replaced it. For a feeling so certain gripped my heart like a vice and held my breath so long that I thought I was about to die.

I was sure that Butterfly was a message. I tried to hope. But several days later I was informed by her family what I already knew; that she was gone. As I dropped the phone onto its stand, I hugged myself for comfort and let my heartfelt tears fall.

Sitting again in the garden, I lean back and close my eyes, and there she is – there we are – throwing our mortar boards. Everyone is jubilant; her parents and mine, her sister and my brother. We stand in groups and cameras click to capture that oh so very special day.

The day we met was the day I was launched into another world like a fledgling from its warm and comfortable nest. I was excited and apprehensive. Having been allotted a room in the University's student dorm, I collected the key and opened the door to my new life, dragging my worldly goods with me. And that's when I met Hoshi. She rose from a chair, bowed in the traditional Japanese way, and with a disarming smile said. "I am very pleased to meet you, I am Hoshi, and I live in the South Island of Japan."

I remember saying something stupid like "Hi, I'm Emily, I live just down the road, in Sussex." She gave a little giggle, and said "I have been waiting for you, so you can please choose the bed of your preference."

Quick to respond, and with fair play in mind, I said. "No, no, you must choose."

Bowing again she said "Very well, I think this one will suit you the best."

With her Japanese ways she was the most delightful person I had ever met, and from that first meeting we were destined to be life long friends.

I still smile, and feel warmth within, thinking of those first weeks. Hoshi somehow managed, in her quiet and gentle way, to convince me that taking off one's shoes before entering a room, and in particular our room, was more practical than cultural. And so it seemed, until it became more difficult as books, keys, and shoes had to be juggled. Finally, on a wet and windy day, our door opened with a crash. Hoshi entered, shoes and all, throwing her bags and books aside and peeling off her dripping coat. She then flopped onto her bed in a heap, shouting, "I give up! I'm ready to be English."

We shared those enlightening years at the centre of university life with laughter and tears. Those years, now a concertina of memories; hours spent searching library shelves, and rushing, always rushing, to lectures. With so many meals of baked beans and omelettes; and our lights on until almost dawn. That is, until Hoshi organised our days, turning off lights and cooking food the Japanese way.

I'm sure I would never have survived if I had shared my room with any other.

So on Graduation day, clutching our degrees, we decided to face the world together. Hoshi had honours in English and English Literature; I completed Economics and Politics.

It was such a happy day, with pure jubilance and joy for all. It was also the day I met her parents and younger sister, who had made the then (and still) peregrine journey, to see Hoshi and share in her accomplishments. A day mortar boards were abandoned skywards, a day of freedom and acknowledgement.

Hoshi had spent many a weekend in my family home and came to be considered part of our family, my parents being as proud of her achievements as they were of mine.

Not that it could overshadow Hoshi's parents, whose delight, I declare, shone like beacons. They had dignity, sincerity and honesty, so visible, that it immediately ensured trust, from all who met them. That was also Hoshi, and it was then I realised why her friendship had so greatly influenced me.

Fate would prove that many would benefit, from and be influenced by Hoshi's unique character. But that was in the future; the present was all we wanted.

With help from our families we rented a small flat in the East End of London. The need to earn a living carried us to numerous interviews, until eventually I got a position as a clerk with an accountant, and Hoshi became an English translator for a Japanese retailer. That small flat became an expression of our joint personalities, and between our mad whirl of clubs and shopping for the latest fashion we spent time making it into a home; a mixture of Japanese style and sixties chic emerged, and for two years we led a carefree and ideal life.

Then it all changed. Hoshi fell in love. We both dated boys, enjoying the flirting and the dating. But this was different, this was very special, and at first I was happy for Hoshi, who believed this young man Richard loved her. And that wedding bells would soon chime.

My lovely gentle friend was so happy, so alive; her eyes full of confidence and love when she told me "Emily, I'm going to have a baby." Then I only felt her joy.

Of course, life isn't all sweetness and roses, although he, Richard, had had them delivered every week for months. I remember summer had given way to blustery winds and falling leaves, when Hoshi's happiness turned to tears, and she sobbed in my arms: "Richard – he isn't ready to be a Father. Or a husband." I held her feeling anger and helplessness. Worse was to come though, for I watched her spirit, her love of life, fade well into winter.

I was sitting quietly with Hoshi one Sunday afternoon when she gave a gasp – a shriek – and feeling her stomach, she gave a look of wonder and with a breathless smile said "The baby moved!" From that moment colour and life came back into her face, and during the following months I often saw her holding her bump with sweet tenderness.

Having given up her work at the retailers, Hoshi worked freelance from the flat; many clients needed her translation skills, so financially she had a secure future for her and the baby.

So it was a shock when she said "Emily, I have decided to go home. I am so very sorry to leave you, but I feel I have no choice."

I had never considered this. "Why? I always thought you knew I would be here for you and the Baby."

She shook her head, "You do not understand Emily; this is the time. I have a family, a country, and I need them, and they also need me. Please understand my dearest friend that my true self has to be in Japan. This time here in England with you and at university is not my reality. It has to end."

"When?" Was all I could say.

"After my baby is born." She then said "I will have to leave the baby. I will have the baby adopted." She didn't look at me. "Please Emily, I will try and make you understand. I was the first girl in my family, in the town, maybe in the whole of South Island, to go to a University in England. So I must return as a success to inspire other young girls. I cannot go back with a child; it would be seen to be a failure. I must make this sacrifice; if I stay I can never leave."

And that is how it was. I don't want to recall the arguments, the reasoning – I tried. To no avail, she went home. The day she left, Hoshi and I hugged, and in tears we vowed to write, a lot. Hoshi, still sobbing, said "Promise me Emily that you will visit me in Japan, and then I can endure this." I promised.

I too went home, stepping back into a familiar life with friends I had always known, and found work that, to my surprise, was gratifying. Hoshi and I did write a lot. Looking back I was often sad; some would say I went through a grieving. Though the years went by; I never forgot my promise and eventually I kept it.

Hoshi became an English teacher, and her letters proved that it became her passion. Within six years of her return to Japan, she received a doctorate and became a professor of English. I could hardly contain my excitement and joy. I made this the opportunity to visit her.

I wanted to take a perfect gift for our reunion; it had to be perfect. And so it was, for having taken shelter from a summer storm in an auction room, I found it; nine inches tall on its wooden stand, a beautiful crystal Butterfly.

I know Hoshi placed it in a window that caught the morning sun, so that each day started with iridescent colour filling her home and, I suspect, thoughts of her child in England, filling her heart.

Hoshi never married, but nevertheless understood my grief, when I became a widow after thirty-seven happy years of marriage; without hesitation, she travelled across the world to comfort me when I needed her the most. My two sons were grown and had long flown the nest. Hoshi came, and stayed until I smiled and laughed again.

She was smaller than I remembered; though her small frame still held a character of herculean strength. She was honoured beyond Japan for her excellence and dedication to her profession; it was well documented and recognised. Even so, I could not help but reflect: was I the only one who knew at what cost?

I have sat too long, I need to prepare some food; for being a Friday, it is the day my eldest son joins me for a long lunch. Today I will have to tell him his Mother has died.

ON THE LINE *by Sharon Black*

Clamped on cotton, side by side,
a spotless sky behind them,
they huddle like newly-weds –

eyes wire-wide, shoulders squared,
feet pointed as they dive:
extreme swimmers suspended against the foam
at the cusp of plummet.

A small pleat is pinched between them –
tight at the fold then a cleft
opening, flaring, disappearing
as it fills with wind.

I crane to see more of the picture –
bed sheet, tablecloth
or length of fabric washed
and ready to be cut to shape –

but the frame obscures the view
leaving me with just a white swathe,
and frantic waving,
high pressure coming in from the east.

BLIND ALLEYS *by Karla Dearsley*

Margaret tried to avoid her reflection in the glass case and concentrate on the ancient shards of painted ceramics within it. The overlay of her sagging face with its untidy wrinkles on the classic sweep of baked clay disturbed her. It was too close to summing up her life; the pure clear beauty she longed for obscured by the messy everyday exterior.

She moved on to the next case, the heels of her court shoes clacking on the parquet floor in a way that made her wince. The attendant looked over and grinned. She nodded back. They were used to her here. She had spent so many lunchtimes at the centre of the web of corridors hidden from life by a barricade of art. She felt conspicuous nonetheless. The high heels and suit, which were supposed to make her feel sophisticated and businesslike, embarrassed her instead. How she longed to take the shoes off and release the trapped toes! She imagined them red and pulsating, as if they had been struck with a hammer in a cartoon.

Easing her weight onto one foot, Margaret took a deep breath and gazed intently at the remains of a Grecian drinking vessel. Coming early was a mistake. Instead of being calmed by the ordered shapes and unbroken stretch of antiquity, Margaret's heart hammered as if stoked with coals to pump hot blood into her cheeks and ears. Would he come? Did she want him to? Such foolishness, and at her age.

She would have to sit down. Margaret took advantage of the next bench, and gazed blankly at the urn in front of her. Meeting here had been her idea. She was not sure why she had chosen the museum and gallery. Perhaps so that she could deny the reason they were together. Was she hoping to fool the world at large, or him? Or herself? Margaret crossed her ankles and allowed one heel to escape its shoe.

On the urn before her a Dionysian celebration was taking place. Satyrs with hairy haunches and protruding tongues chased immodest nymphs with breasts and thighs carelessly displayed around the clay frieze. Or was it the other way around? The circular design made it hard to tell. Maybe the satyrs only chased because the nymphs ran, the action an invitation that could later be disclaimed.

Madness. Margaret was on dangerous ground: a middle-aged academic with only a few more terms to go before she could enjoy an early retirement, contemplating starting a fling with a student, and an unpromising one at that in whatever sense she chose to look at him. Jez's unpunctuality, jumbled notes and rumpled appearance showed him to be hopelessly disorganised. At first she had thought the attraction was merely a matter of frustrated maternal instinct, but she had come across plenty of other hopeless students over the years and she did not need the sensation between her legs that made her shift in her seat and lose track of her sentence whenever he was in the class, to know that this was different.

For a whole term she had avoided having to acknowledge the uncomfortable truth. The seminars were well attended and the greatest risk she ran was that of having to squeeze past him in a doorway or crowded corridor. When she allowed herself to look, Margaret saw how solitary he was and the recognition in his eyes. Then came the end of term tutorials.

"You have some good ideas, Jeremy..."

"Jez, please."

She had sighed at the interruption, at her most stern and brisk. "... but your work is messy. Think ahead before you start."

Good advice was rarely followed, especially by the one who offered it, and Margaret had been no exception. Inevitably, Jez had dropped his papers when he stood to leave, and inevitably, their hands and eyes had met as she had helped retrieve them. Her lips could still feel his soft, tentative kiss, and the pressure of her response.

Margaret caught herself about to shake her head, and glanced quickly at the other pot-gazers. No one was looking in her direction, and if they had been their gaze would no doubt have slid beyond her or to one side as if she did not exist. Her ignorability had long irritated her. It allowed flashier academics to race past her and her meticulous plodding achievements on the promotion trail. Perhaps that was why Jez had made an impact on her. He actually saw her, saw 'her'. At least, that was what she wanted to believe.

Curbing the urge to look at her watch, Margaret contemplated the urn once more. How inconvenient it must have been for satyrs, and all those other half-human, half-beast creations of the ancients, to have their untamed 'other' proclaimed by their appearance. Like the adolescent students, who had yet to gain control of their hormones and their facial hair. Like Jez, uncertain how to behave, vulnerable and looking to her for guidance, wanting to dominate.

"Explain it to me," he had said.

She knew his understanding of the role of the Chorus in Greek drama needed no extra input from her, but she had taken him at his word and explained. "The Greeks used drama to tame the passions and make them safe. The audience poured out its anger and frustration with those on stage. They went home to be responsible wives and husbands, mothers and fathers."

As with drama, so with pots. Acts of bestiality, orgies of greed and passion were revealed to the looker and contained. They could be analysed from a safe distance, trapped in clay. The museum placed another layer – one of glass – between the dispassionate viewer and the dangerous emotions beneath.

It was a good place for thinking. She was safe here from all that could hurt her, whether civilisation or chaos. Margaret sighed. She scrutinised the expression on one of the nymph's faces. The smile and tilt of the chin spoke of expectation rather than fear. The disposition of the limbs and flow of her scanty garments was too elegant to be haphazard. She had released her passion, welcomed it, not been overcome by it. She did not fear it as Margaret did. Suppose that she lost herself – or found herself?

Margaret stood abruptly, ignoring her aching toes and looked for a way out. If she headed for the main exit she risked bumping into Jez, but the stairs would only lead her deeper into the building. Which way to go? She had been down blind alleys too many times before. Her own student days had been full of them. Her looks then were pleasant, but could have been stunning if she had ever got the knack of feeling comfortable in dolly-girl make-up and a mini skirt. When Guy had started paying her attention she had been flattered. He had the kind of groovy persona, proclaimed by his droopy moustache and Afghan coat, that made him admired by both girls and boys. After a couple of dates and white hot kisses Margaret's pulse played a samba rhythm whenever he entered the room. Then came the day when she was called to the lecturer's office and accused of plagiarism.

"You surely don't expect me to believe that you hit upon the same arguments as Guy by accident? It's well known on the campus that you've been courting."

"But... " Margaret's cheeks became rosy again at the memory. She had not wanted to get Guy into trouble, but could not get herself out of it unless she did. She did not blame the lecturer for not believing her, she could hardly believe it herself until she had confronted Guy with it. His laughter stung her as if she had been slapped.

"Sure I copied your essay – you don't seriously think I'd be seen with a square chick like you for any other reason."

Passion meant humiliation; it was that simple. She would not fly, like the nymph and risk Jez reading her action as encouragement. She would wait calmly and when Jez arrived she would direct him in cool tones to study the scene drawn on the clay and learn from it. Margaret allowed herself a glance at her watch. Late! She sank back onto the bench. How irritating! Didn't he realise how busy she was? Margaret clamped her teeth shut to stop her lip trembling. Maybe humiliation was closer than she had thought. So many blind alleys and here she was right back at the start again.

Margaret caught sight of a tousled figure and her breath snagged. Then he turned and her smile faded. Not Jez. Nothing like him really. He strode into the room as if it had been created for him. His glance swept over Margaret barely registering her presence. She might have been another antique exhibit, devoid of life and interest. Margaret felt an urge to climb on the bench and start singing 'Hey, Big Spender!' to see his expression of astonishment, but she kept her gaze fixed on the urn, her hands neatly folded in her lap.

Round and round they went; nymphs and satyrs, satyrs and nymphs, their passion never consummated, in an unending circle from which they could never break free. There was only one way to escape the frenzy. Repression did not work, all that did was allow the beast to charge out of the shadows when it was least expected. The path might meander, but unless she wanted to spend all her lunchtimes sitting here gazing at unfulfilled passions she had to move on.

A face suddenly appeared sideways from behind the pot, framed by the case. Jez looked comical, a mixture of pride and uncertainty.

"Hi there. Sorry I'm late. Have you been waiting long?"

"Only about twenty years."

"Nice pot," he grinned.

Margaret pulled a face. She stood and took his hand. "Come on, let me show you the Impressionists."

They took a few steps towards the door, then Margaret stopped and removed her shoes. Swinging them by their heels from one hand and with his hand in the other, Margaret took Jez to find an Elysian field where they could let the beast run free.

SHRINK *by Sharon Keating*

The swifts shriek me home
across the sand, through marram grass
and dunes, across low-lying land
where clumps of cattle graze, steadfast

free-flowing, ruddy as a fistful of loam.
Where you mumble your roan muzzle
into my palm; submerge me in the harbour-lights
of your pony-eyed pools. I feed you

polo mints, fresh as your hay-breath,
leaning into you; a quiver to a bow. Rub
your neck-pelt as you crunch and stamp
and blow warm breezes, snorting shrink-dried

teasels, grass seeds, hemp. Large as a hay-wagon,
measured just now, slow. As if this, this moment
looped over a gate, has always been, will last forever.
Never go.

Coastal waters won't hesitate; fields just waiting
anticipating open pastures streaming with kelp,
nuzzled by sea-cows and under-water-horses.
Nothing holds. No

recompense for overwhelming sea defences
(thatched marram grass, knotted roots woven
through dunes). Whale-deep, the North Sea broods.
Lumbersome sharks lurk, wild sea-trout, krill

triplets of bottle-nosed apostrophes punctuate
above their reach. Old pachyderm is patient;
slate skin wrinkling, creasing, folding always
into an infinity of pleats.

AN EQUATION FOR JUSTICE *by Michael Roe*

For every beginning there is an end. Death is a function of birth. The only variables are where, when and how.

You scan the unfamiliar bedroom; mouth dry, breathing laboured. You slump into a chair away from the window, drop the gun into your lap and check your watch. Twelve minutes past six. Outside, a dying sun bleeds on slate rooftops. Rhythmic chants of children filter through part open window. They laugh. You smile. A man's voice. 'Siobhan, Marie, Michael! Will y'no come in now! Y'mammy's got your dinner on the table, so she has!' Chants crumble to hopeless protest. You smell the fish and chips that you imagine sits on the family table and your stomach rumbles. Memories of happier times.

The street is silent.

He will be home before eight after two pints of Guinness at Kelly's bar. Yes, you have done your homework. Your mind roams; Good Friday Agreement plus political expedience equals injustice. And the anger wells up inside you like heartburn. Maybe it is needed. Needed to stifle the humanity.

Humanity. Love. God, how you miss JoJo and the girls. You squeeze your eyes shut and feel the well of tears that seep like melting ice from tired lids.

Voices make their way up the street. They stop nearby in mumbled conversation. A man laughs. Your hands tremble, jaw locks, heart races. Right hand slides around the butt of the pistol as your mind swirls in the mist of the nightmare. Conversation dies. A front door slams. And the tick-tick-tick of a single pair of steel-tipped heels fades into the dusk. Neck muscles loosen, shoulders drop. The grip on the pistol slackens. You breathe again.

The room has become stuffy. You push wisps of hair from your face. A trickle of sweat from your armpit slides down your body, and you shudder. It was a day much like today; sunny, warm, airless. An Indian summer, some had called it. The class had been contemplating their new maths curriculum when a colleague entered the classroom and whispered in your ear. You knew it was serious; a request from the Head to meet in his office mid lesson was not his style. "An accident" was the way he had put it. An accident? Being in the wrong place at the wrong time when a bomb goes off is an accident? But all you remember is the numbness in your brain, the heaviness of your limbs. Now, after two years of planning, a Browning semiautomatic pistol nestles in your lap as snug as a new kitten.

Somewhere in the house timbers creak. Your heart flutters. Concentrate! Concentrate! You turn your head towards the partly open door that hangs like a spectre in the gathering gloom. But nothing moves. It was just the sigh of a tired old house.

A voice in the distance. He is singing. And as he gets closer you make out a tune. The voice is soothing, almost enchanting. He sings of his love for a girl from County Clare. He stops. He is close. A key grinds into the lock of the front door. You can almost hear the thump-thump-thump inside your chest. For a moment your head swims. Think cold; think logic; think next line. You grip the Browning and push yourself up off the chair.

Front door shudders. Television chatters into life. He is still singing. A clatter of plates. It is time. Time to right the wrong. For JoJo, your friend, your lover, your confidante; for your beautiful Susie and Scarlet. Your eyes blur. You bite your lip. Think mathematics; think cold; think next line.

You squeeze through the part open doorway, take a deep breath, release the Browning's safety catch and ease yourself, step by step, down towards the dull light at the foot of the stairs. To the right, a wall mirror flickers television light. To the left, on a small table just inside the lounge sits a photograph of a little blond girl holding hands with a young couple. The couple smile; the little girl laughs. Probably Scarlet's age when ....

The target is in the kitchen, judging by the light that seeps into the lounge. Still he sings, as the microwave beeps and whirs.

And then the telephone rings.

Finger tightens on the trigger of the Browning. You swallow hard and flatten your aching back against the wall. He picks up the phone from the lounge and carries it to the kitchen.

'Hello!' he says, and pauses. 'Now that wouldn't be Daddy's favourite little girl in the whole wide world would it be?'

You ease round so that your back is against the front door. A side step; the small table nudges your right leg; and the target is in view. He has his back to you. It's easy. Oh so easy. You hold the Browning in both hands, spread your feet, flex your knees and slowly raise your arms.

'Oh! Is it your birthday now? Ah! And there's me thinking it's next year, so I did!' He leans on the kitchen sink as the television blares out the signature tune of Coronation Street.

A sudden flicker of television light hits the mirror. A quick glance, and you gasp. The image is barely recognisable. Your hair is damp and tangled, face knotted with hatred and fear. Bloodshot eyes set in sunken sockets have run mascara trails down your cheeks. You turn back to face him. Is it justice, or is it revenge? Does it matter? Yes! No! No! Sweat seems to ooze from every pore of your body. Think cold; think logic; think next line.

'Present, y'say?' He chuckles. 'Might have one around the house somewhere! Only if y'mammy says you've been a good girl, now.'

You lick your parched lips. Just squeeze the trigger and the pain will go. But will it? Will it only double the pain factor by inserting yet another innocent into the equation? You feel your arms dropping. But it must balance. The equation must balance. What is done to one side must be done to the other; that is the perfection of mathematics! You raise the gun again. It is heavy and harsh in your hands. You feel the pressure of trigger against finger. What would JoJo say? *How can you bring back something that is already lost?* But, an eye for an eye? *What would be gained except more pain, more bitterness!*

Your teeth bite into your lower lip and you taste the blood. Bitter, bitter blood.

You take one hand from the gun, reach inside your leather jacket, pull out that last precious photo and place it next to the framed picture of the couple and pretty little blonde girl. You lower the Browning, remove its magazine without taking your eyes off the man in the kitchen, and place the magazine on top of your photo. You reach blindly for the front door catch, ease the door open, slip the gun into the inside pocket of your leather jacket, and step backwards into the night. You begin to run. The air is sweet and fresh in your lungs. And you run; and you run; and you run.

2013

THE JUDGES 2013

In 2013, our Short Story category judge was Julia Churchill, formerly of Greenhouse and now of AM Heath Publishers. She had this to say about her experience of working with the Yeovil Literary Prize:

'...It's always such a thrill to judge a competition and I wasn't disappointed. There are some great voices and stories here, and they've stayed with me for long after the judging.'

Neil Astley of Bloodaxe Books was our Poetry category judge for 2013 and had this to say about the standard of the entries:

'...what I hadn't realised was that the overall quality of the entries would be so high...'

'...each to be tasted again and again to try and identify those with the fullest and most subtle flavour.'

Of his chosen winners, he commented:

'All three poems are so good that it feels unfair to make them first, second and third. I feel they are all winners.'

The Yeovil Literary Prize

2013 Prizewinners

First

Kiran Millwood Hargrave *Grace*	99
Chip Tolson *Let It Be Anthea*	100

Second

Chrissy Banks *The Waves*	104
Janet Hancock *Homecoming*	105

Third

Sandra Galton *With Hindsight*	110
Elizabeth McLaren *Lola the Corolla*	111

GRACE *by Kiran Millwood Hargrave*

1st Prizewinner

In the moments of his leaving himself
    his hands shook and could not take mine.

Instead he stared
    and handed through the silence

the slightest cup of my chin
    rolled my cheeks between his fingers

like dough, and in those seconds
    he still needed me,

and it was a blessing as complete as bread.

Inside the night-time minutes
    he held me with this gaze

until the slender tap of knuckle
    at his throat wound back and down.

I touched my palms in prayer
    to stay the longer held in that stare

as the trimmed nail of his tongue
    lay still, and settled clasped into its last-grasp.

LET IT BE ANTHEA *by Chip Tolson*

1ˢᵗ Prizewinner

She pushes ahead to find the reserved seat making sure I settle and can see my suitcase stowed at the end of the carriage, checks I have my magazine and picnic box and tells me to wait before eating the sandwiches; it's a long journey. After a quick kiss she's off the train with only moments to spare before we're pulling away from Leeds on the early morning cross country bound for Plymouth.

Morag mothers me. It's not as if I've never caught a train before. I guess it's what daughters do when their fathers grow old and live on their own. Not like my twice divorced son Alec now a professor at Plymouth University, he's at a conference all day and too busy to meet my train. I'm to take a taxi to his house where the door key is under a brick beside the front step.

I don't think Morag realises I'm in a 'Quiet' carriage. This new mobile is complicated not simply a phone like the old one. Given the 'smart phone' for my birthday I have to make the best of it. As I fiddle it flashes and a photo of my tray table appears on its screen before, with a bleep, it turns off.

I don't like reading with the train rocking. I watch the industrial landscape of South Yorkshire slip by, its new business estates set amongst crumbling buildings of past labouring generations before it gives way to Midland farmlands with their fields ready for harvest.

Dozing I'm woken by a knock against my seat, a snack trolley is passing along the carriage stacked with cans, pasties, sandwiches and chocolate bars. We haven't got to Birmingham and I've eaten my picnic. I buy a beer, but I ask for a beaker, I don't fancy drinking out of the can.

I'm eager to be travelling across Somerset again looking out for anywhere I recognise from my youth, years culminating in my days as a cub reporter on the County Gazette. Later I was off to National Service, to the army in Germany before pounding countless streets as an ever more experienced if not always appreciated reporter on regional papers, a married man with growing children.

Bristol, wet and grimy, gives a glimpse of Brunel's suspension bridge. I reported on a suicide off that bridge. With high tide in the river the young woman survived her fall to be pulled clear of the water in shock only to die in hospital hours later. They never found her next of kin or any note of why she did it.

The train gathers speed across farmland dotted with grazing cows over the flat land of the Levels and before I realise how far we've travelled we pull into the remembered scene of the station with the longest platforms on the once proud Great Western Railway, platforms where I stood in short trousers by hissing steam giants reeking grease and coal dust after their haul down from Paddington. We kids, I was never alone, were always hoping to get an invite onto the footplate the name and number of the engine already written down. That well-thumbed notebook is in a box on top of my bedroom wardrobe. I never mention it to anyone.

Nothing happens after the hubbub of arrival and intending departure settles down. The Guard, I still call them Guards, comes on the tannoy announcing a delay due to a rostering problem. A few minutes later he comes through the carriage telling us a relief driver is on his way on an incoming train, but he won't be with us for quarter of an hour. Across the platform I see a sign still painted in Great Western colours: Gentlemen. It'll be a better opportunity than the over used compartment on board. He agrees I have time and to take a stroll along the platform.

My wandering takes me through the booking hall, remembered but modernised, no longer polished Victorian hardwood now glass and electronic screens, and out into the station forecourt. Across the road the Gaiety Cinema, the home of countless Saturday morning adventures, is now a snooker hall. The young man on the door says I can only enter if I'm going to play. The Duty Supervisor is more amenable and I get to look inside and tell her about the days of Roy Rogers and Trigger on the black and white screen.

Back at the station the downline track is vacant, the train and my suitcase travelling on to Plymouth sooner than expected and my dalliance too long chatting by the pool tables.

I give my details: "Mr James Crosswell, Coach A, Seat 51B", and luggage description to be sent down the line to Plymouth. I'm told to contact the Duty Manager on arrival and given the times of the afternoon's trains, one every hour. Time looking round old haunts in my childhood town is more enticing than twiddling my thumbs waiting for Alec's conference to finish.

The shops along Station Road have changed, gone is Mrs Palmer with her shelves laden with fruit and vegetables and the Novelty Joke Shop, a favourite haunt of kids without pocket money to the fury of Mr Norris, is a kebab house. Stillman's the Butcher is the only place unchanged. I can't imagine how many tons of beef have passed over those marble slabs in the intervening years.

Further into town once petrol fumed streets are pedestrian spaces interrupted by bleeping tones from backing delivery vans. Too many town centre shops have whitewashed windows displaying faded closing down sale signs for there to be any buzz about the place. And it starts to rain.

I'm lucky to avoid the storm judging by the sleet rattling the windows and people rushing in wearing soaking coats. I'm at a table with my order taken for coffee and a pastry, the spare chairs from my table taken to make up numbers at another. Early customers are surprised at the unexpected rush as two waitresses work to keep up with new orders.

The building has gone through transformations since its Victorian beginnings as a meeting hall now a cafe serving meals to lunchtime office staff and shoppers. A space extends from the tables to the street doors showing the original woodblock floor dampened by the rush of folk coming in from the storm.

Teenage years spent in this hall with French chalked floors surge into my mind. Mother insisted I go to dancing lessons and I came to this place, hanging back against the wall with rain soaked trousers from bicycling to my lesson until Miss Mountjoy called me out to introduce myself to one of the girls, it was always a taller girl.

'Let it be Anthea' I whispered to myself every time Miss Mountjoy's all seeing eyes cast round the hall pairing up her pupils. Anthea was my age, well three weeks older to be precise – I glimpsed the register one evening and kept repeating her birth date all the way home determined to send her a card when the day came. Her father brought and collected her by car it was never damp clothes for Anthea. During the second winter of our classes we were often picked out to demonstrate to the class responding to Miss Mountjoy's running commentary, but in all that time we hardly spoke. She didn't return for the third winter, I'd only signed up in the hope of seeing her there again. And she never acknowledged the birthday card I slipped through the letterbox of her parents' detached house on the well-off side of town bicycling away in the dark hoping not to be seen.

A queue forms, hopeful customers looking for tables. I sit tight the rain still heavy, there's no hurry with so many trains to finish my journey. Across the room a woman sits staring at her plate, a man and a woman, maybe a married son or daughter, sit either side of her trying to get her to engage and eat her slice of cake.

Could it be?

I push back my chair and walk over. 'Anthea?'

She doesn't react. Concerned the man and woman stare at me.

'Anthea, it is you, isn't it?' I know she hears me. Sixty years may have passed yet as she turns lifting her head her eyes are the same eyes I could never look into without blushing.

'James, is it our turn again?'

The rhythm is in my mind yet we share it. She stands pressing her hand down on the table to hold her balance.

'Mother, are you all right?'

'James has asked me to dance, Michael. He's such a polite boy.'

No longer are her eyes above mine. As if classes were yesterday we take each other in a formal hold and slowly move into the room as queuing customers ease back clearing the floor.

We don't speak. Minutes pass, the man and woman at Anthea's table look on in amazement as we circle round at our slow pace then they stand and applaud, tears running down her son's cheeks as I guide Anthea back to her table, our dance done.

'I enjoyed your birthday card, James. It was thoughtful of you. Come on, Michael, there's no call for tears when you see me dancing.' Seated she turns away back into her staring state.

Michael drives me to Taunton station. We're greeted on the platform by a Manager newly on shift.

'Everyone is looking for you, Mr Crosswell. There's a proper fuss going on. Your son went to meet you at Plymouth and you weren't on any trains. He and your daughter in Leeds have been trying to ring you. Any longer and we would have got the police involved for a missing person enquiry.'

'But my son couldn't meet me, he's at a conference.'

'He was at the station to meet you, Mr Crosswell. Next departure for Plymouth is in five minutes, you better be on it and turn your phone on, please. There'll be messages waiting.'

Michael looks on. 'I'm sorry about the fuss, Mr Crosswell.'

'It'll blow over. I did enjoy meeting Anthea... your mother, again. I hope I haven't upset her.'

'What a tonic you've given her. Who'd have thought it, sixty years gone by and she knew you as if it was yesterday. There are days she doesn't know me.' Michael blinks, 'and I didn't know she could dance. It's the best day she's had in years.'

We shake hands before I look through jacket pockets for my phone.

THE WAVES *by Chrissy Banks*

2nd Prizewinner

You say the city pavements are choppy
with ice. Snow spits at your face, flies
at huddles of the homeless. Alone
in the building long after midnight,
you try to calm the stranger with Jesus hair
just two steps away from you. He plunges
hands in his pockets to feel for something
hidden. You know tonight, again,
you will not sleep. Everyone is sinking,
everyone signed off sooner or later.
Sometimes you call in sick, but only when
you talk about drowning is anyone
nervous enough to listen. So you tell them
about the waves, how sometimes
one rears up high as a house. They say
if you can't stay afloat, get out of the water,
let someone else do the job. And you look
at the gentle faces on the poster on the wall;
you look out of the window at Rosanne,
nineteen, half-naked, trying to suck warmth
from a roll-up; you look at the closed door
of the manager's face, the wave, suspended,
high over your head. You can feel
your face breaking, imagine walking out,
picking your way over the treacherous ice
on a one-way trek through the city.
Then, with an inward breath, you think again
of that bus driver yesterday, who stopped,
climbed out of his cab, to help
a blind man in a swirling sea of traffic.

HOMECOMING *by Janet Hancock*

2nd Prizewinner

IT was at the cheese counter in Pricerite that Melanie knew she was going to marry Street Hooper. I mean, who would call their son Street? Ma Hooper, everybody supposed, although Melanie was probably the only one who ever found out why. 'Streetie,' you'd hear when he was small if you were along the lane past the open back door; sometimes, 'Sweetie'; and, yes, 'Streetie, Sweetie.' In the school playground, any lad who tried those names felt the force of Street's fist. But Street was good with catapults, and punctures and fixing things, and it was best to have him on your side.

Street's daddy did not exist; had never been.

In their seventeenth summer, Melanie and Street ambled along the lane from school, the inch between their hands a chasm neither dared cross, air surrounding them fragrant with wood smoke, bursting with possibility, a Garden of Eden, ripe fruit waiting to be plucked. Sometimes they met Ma Hooper. She would stare at them, eyes like currants, set in a face that made Melanie think of pickled walnuts somebody gave her family one Christmas, black hair swept under a kerchief tied at the back, and hoop earrings. Melanie thought she might have been a gypsy. Ma Hooper always had a sprig of heather in the top buttonhole of her dress, just visible above her pinafore.

'A bookish girl, she is, Street,' Ma Hooper said once, as if Melanie were not there. 'She'll be off before long.'

'Marry me, Mel,' Street said to her the summer of their eighteenth year as they lay in the grass beyond the village, clear stream water whispering over pebbles, the swish of reeds and call of curlews their only company. By now, hands had touched, legs entwined, lips brushing lips, cotton against restraining cotton. She placed fingertips on his unblemished face weathered the colour of caramel from hours of digging drains and ditches; brushed from his forehead light brown hair which summer seemed to kiss with golden lights. The only thing of his mother's he had were eyes so dark a brown as to be black.

'I've my scholarship, Street.'

'I'll wait for you,' he said, as if talking about the school gate not the next three years of her life. She was going to read history at university. Hundreds of miles away in London.

She thought of the absent daddy; had even asked him once. 'M'daddy,' Street had sighed, looked at some point known only to himself, smiled, added, 'God bless him, for only God knows.'

She forgot about Street's daddy; wondered if this was love, this need and yet contentment to lie and touch and kiss and drowse, and gaze at another's face; and if it was love, was it only something for the young and free, not for parents, her mother and father with three other girls, workworn farm hands, never a moment to themselves.

The train to London carried her away from Street, the rhythm of wheels on rails lulling her to sleep: *Marry me, Mel; Marry me, Mel.*

First time home, for Christmas, she found he'd left the village. 'Gone to look for work,' said the next sister down from her, a knowing glint in her eye. 'Best forget him, Melly.'

What did Rosa think there was to remember? For Melanie had never talked about Street. Rosa was in a solicitor's office in town, shorthand and typing two evenings a week, and walking out with a boy from the gas showrooms who roared up the lane on a motorbike.

The wind swept in from the North Sea, rattling doors and windows. Melanie put on an extra sweater, shut herself in her room with a one-bar electric fire to read about nineteenth century British Colonial policy; wrote an essay on Cecil Rhodes; glimpsed a wider horizon. The walls of the farmhouse, her parents' tired faces, all seemed to ask *what now?*

Back in London, that spring and summer she bought a mini skirt, and boots that laced up to her thighs; had her hair cut, backcombed it, learned to use mascara; discovered vodka and lime, passion, the ecstatic moment, the emptiness of another dawn. She attended talks on Africa, volunteering, and armed with a degree that was better than she'd expected went to work in Northern Rhodesia, administration in a rural hospital up country, stayed on after independence and the new name, Zambia.

She didn't need to walk down the lane. Her parents – their other daughters all married - had sold the farm, bought a bungalow on the edge of town. She stood for a moment looking at her old home; the new owners had replaced the doors and windows. Before climbing back into the little Deux Chevaux, which had cost her ten pounds and always reminded her of an upside down wheelbarrow, she would continue as far as the river. Ma Hooper was in her garden picking daffodils, hair now quite white, still the sprig of heather in her top buttonhole, perhaps the same one as years ago.

Ma Hooper looked up. 'Well, see what the wind's blown in.'
'Hello, Mrs Hooper.'

Ma Hooper regarded her, Melanie conscious of how different she must look: ankle-length batik skirt, African drop earrings of three small wooden cubes. 'Lost weight, you have,' Ma Hooper commented, 'not that there was any to lose.'

She smiled. 'Africa ... you know,' although she didn't see how Ma Hooper could know; didn't see how to begin to describe to her or anybody ten years of sunsets that took the breath away, of eyes eloquent with desperation, resignation, gratitude, of wide open spaces, cooking fires and spicy smells, and the rhythmical hum of women's voices. 'I had malaria,' she said.

'Hot was it there?'

'You could say.'

'Time for the kettle on?'

She nodded, used to hospitality, usually from people who had nothing. 'Thank you.'

She paused on the threshold of the back door. She'd never been inside. Ma Hooper waved a hand and Melanie sat at the deal table on a ladder-backed chair, a faded paisley cushion tied to the seat.

Ma Hooper filled the kettle, put the daffodils in a tall thin vase of mauve glass. 'It's prison, he's in,' she volunteered, her back to Melanie.

'I'm sorry.'

Ma Hooper brought strong tea in rose patterned china cups, more of which, with plates, decorated a Welsh dresser along one wall. She pushed the sugar towards Melanie, watched while she heaped several spoonfuls into her cup. 'Grievous bodily harm,' Ma Hooper said, as if repeating something learned by rote at school, words whose feel on her tongue she was getting used to. 'I call it a fight. Unexpectedly. But that's temper, isn't it? Like his daddy. That's why his mama ran away.' Ma Hooper glanced up as if she would gauge Melanie's reaction. 'You thought I was his ma, didn't you? Everybody did. No reason not to.'

'Does he know?'

Ma Hooper shook her head. 'He was only a baby. And his mama wasn't much more than a girl, my little sister.'

'I used to wonder about his name. Street,' Melanie ventured.

Ma Hooper shrugged. 'A place, somewhere they were going to settle, she and ...' Ma Hooper stopped, as if to speak the name of Street's daddy would give the man a dignity, a humanity, he did not deserve. 'He filled her head with a lot of nonsense before he hit it.' Ma Hooper drank some tea, looked at the table. 'Street needs a steady girl behind him. I shan't be here for ever. He should be out in the summer.'

Ma Hooper took Melanie's cup to refill it. When she returned to the table, Melanie confronted sadness in those currant eyes, a face for whom life held no surprises.

'Shrewsbury prison,' Ma Hooper said. 'Too far to visit.' Tears teetered on wrinkled skin and Melanie put a hand over a wizened claw.

His hair was flecked with white and he took off wire-rimmed spectacles as he stood, bent to greet her across the table in the green-emulsioned visiting room.

'Mel.' He kissed her on the cheek.

'Hooper!' a warder yelled. 'No physical contact with visitors.'

They stepped back, the air between them waiting, as it had done when they were seventeen. She breathed the masculine smell of tobacco, and a whiff of soap, momentarily replacing the cloying one of disinfectant. A butterfly fluttered inside her, that perhaps he had made an effort, for she had written to say she would be there. *Mel.* Nobody else had called her that. *Marry me, Mel. Marry me, Mel.*

They sat down, looked at each other. Blue prison clothes hung loosely on him and there was a greyish pallor about his indoor skin. She wondered if he, too, was asking himself how to fill the gaps of nearly fifteen years, jigsaw shapes scattered on the floor. She parted her lips with no idea which words were lining themselves up, yet could not let half an hour's visiting pass in silence.

Street spoke before her. 'I'm studying,' he told her. 'This new Open University. History of Art. I want to see them, Mel.' Hunger, need, lit his eyes. 'All those masterpieces. Not just in a book.'

'We'll go together,' she said.

'Come the summer?'

She nodded, imagined the little car, roof down, wind through their hair as they started to piece together the jigsaw.

'You know what I miss, Mel?' he said across the table the following week. 'Cheese. Funny, isn't it?'

Ma Hooper said she'd go with Melanie next visit. Sometimes, Ma Hooper went with her in the Deux Chevaux to Pricerite, otherwise gave her a list. 'You can stay here, you know, have his room till he comes back,' Ma Hooper told her, helping carry bags from the car.

But Melanie returned each time to her bedsit in town; could just afford it and the car with her job at the Council offices.

The day before Street's release she stood by the cheese counter. Gorganzola. Shiny, crumbly, veined blue-green as if afflicted by some alien sickness. She couldn't remember having any before.

'Want to try some?' a girl in a pink overall indicated a plate on the counter.

She put the small cube in her mouth, closed her eyes, moved her tongue over the creamy bitterness of the cheese. She wondered if he would enjoy it; and, like a flower opening towards the sun's warmth, embraced all the things they were going to learn or rediscover.

WITH HINDSIGHT *by Sandra Galton*

3rd Prizewinner

It would be the very last time
you breathed in the air of the room you loved, you knew
so well. The Gillray Prints appeared unmoved, considering:
might return be an option? You had come downstairs unaided
bearing the pain, the joy from your past life, hovered unsure
this was the moment to leave. With memories rejuvenated
your eyes opened wide, and wider to absorb, acknowledge
each item. Once in the room, familiarity made you smile. 'Still
here now?' you whispered - a rhetorical question, touching
my heart with shame. I looked away. 'The ambulance is
coming.' 'So soon then?' you said. 'It's ok, this place?' It's only
when you thanked me I wanted to stop that ambulance.
I wasn't sure what to do.

I wasn't sure what to do
when you thanked me. I wanted to stop that ambulance
coming so soon. Then you said 'It's ok; this place - it is only
my heart.' With shame I looked away. 'The ambulance is
here now.' You whispered a rhetorical question, touching
each item once in the room. Familiarity made you smile still;
your eyes opened wide, and wider to absorb. Acknowledge
this was the moment: to leave with memories rejuvenated,
bearing the pain, the joy from your past. Life hovered, unsure -
might return be an option? You had come downstairs unaided
so well; the Gillray Prints appeared unmoved considering...
You breathed in the air of the room you loved. You knew
it would be the very last time.

LOLA THE COROLLA *by Elizabeth McLaren*

3rd Prizewinner

Ruby's evening starts out just fine. She gives Ryan his dinner early and packs him off to band practice, with his precious saxophone on the back seat of the old Toyota Corolla - his first solo journey.

To celebrate the demise of the parental taxi service, Paul has offered to make dinner, just for the two of them. He uncorks a bottle of red with a flourish (one of his special ones from the bottom row of the wine rack) pours Ruby a glass and instructs her to go off for a soak in the bath while he prepares the meal. Steak and oven chips with salad, his signature dish - well actually his only dish, but at least she shopped for the steak so there is a possibility it won't be like the proverbial piece of old shoe leather.

Ruby lies in the scented bath with her book and wine, willing herself to relax. The smoke alarm goes off. She persuades herself to be only mildly irritated by this intrusion and the accompanying howling from the dog. It only goes off once – probably a record for her husband cooking a steak. She smiles to herself at the vision of Paul and Rufus their red setter leaping around the kitchen, Paul flapping a tea towel at the alarm and the dog's ears flapping in imitation. She guesses this is her signal to get out of the bath, put on comfy pyjamas and get downstairs for dinner.

Indulgent she knows; but they sit down in front of the TV with their meal on trays and pour another glass of wine. Paul wants to watch a movie, with Angelina Jolie, and since it also has James McAvoy in, she doesn't bother to argue. Even though it means she's missing Masterchef.

The steak is good. Very good. Crusty, peppery and charred on the outside, still crimson and bloody in the middle. Just how she likes it.

Paul raises his glass in a toast, 'To Ryan and to freedom! His and ours. No more school run and no more late nights picking him up from stuff.'

Ruby just nods, as her mouth is full and clinks her glass against his.

Paul carries on, 'First go as well. Pretty good, eh. Not many boys pass first time. Course he couldn't have done it without you. I don't know how you had the patience to give him all those lessons. I couldn't have done it.'

No, you couldn't, thinks Ruby, remembering all those drives down the winding road into town, to Ryan's sixth form college. Just sitting there, supposedly teaching Ryan to drive, her fists surreptitiously clenched together in her lap, hidden under her handbag. Fighting the urge to keep saying 'Slow down!' as he threw the car round the corners like a rally driver.

'I know he thinks dear old Lola is a bit of a bus. A bit of a granny car,' says Paul, 'but at least we know she's safe. She's been serviced every year and all checked over when he turned seventeen. When he's a bit older he can get himself something flash. I've got the company car, so perhaps we could get you something smarter to drive now.'

'That would be nice,' says Ruby, while thinking that what he really means is they should get something he would like to drive at weekends.

By the end of the movie Paul is nodding. The wine makes him do funny little grunting snores and Ruby thinks to herself that he is looking old. He wakes up for the News at Ten, but after the weather (turning colder as the night goes on – danger of icy patches on the roads after the showers earlier) he gets up, leans over the back of the sofa and kisses her on the top of her head. 'I'm off up now. Got to be down to Plymouth by nine tomorrow. It's going to be a long day. Can you make sure you put Rufus out for a pee?'

Ruby stops up for a while, watching the local news, then tidies away the dishes and puts the dishwasher on. Funny how when Paul cooks he never clears away. She rinses the glasses and leaves them to drain. She opens the back door to let the dog out and stands on the patio in her slippers looking up at the clear sky, watching her breath frosting in the air. The words 'turning colder' and 'icy patches' keep running through her head.

Ruby calls the dog back in and locks and bolts the back door. She knows Ryan will come through the front door as they have just had his own key cut for him. She shuts Rufus away in the utility room. Most nights she'd just give him a pat and tell him to go to bed, but tonight she gives the dog a hug and a treat and fusses him for a few moments. She checks to make sure the outside lights are on at the front of the house so Ryan is not fumbling about in the dark to find the keyhole. She dries the glasses with a tea towel, polishing them till they sparkle and then puts them away in the cupboard. She can't make herself go to bed.

Looking around for something else to do, she checks the clothes on the drying rack by the AGA. Dry enough. So she sorts and folds them into neat piles, which she stacks up and carries up the stairs. So as not to disturb Paul, she leaves their clothes on the bed in the spare room but takes Ryan's pile into his room.

Having put the clothes away in the drawers, Ruby picks up a damp towel off the floor and sits down on the bed clutching it in her lap. She looks around the room, her gaze falling on the Blood Sweat and Beers poster. She imagines Ryan as he was this afternoon, standing in the kitchen, leaning on the counter in his skinny jeans, telling her in deadly seriousness, 'You know, Mum, New Riot really are probably the best up and coming ska/punk band in the country. You ought to listen to them'. Maybe she will.

Ryan has left his computer on. Maybe he's still signed in to Facebook. Or perhaps Ruby could just check his Google history to see what he is up to. You hear such bad things about kids and the Internet. But she doesn't look. She trusts Ryan. Yes, she tells herself, she really does.

She's not so sure about that Thomas boy though. Bit of a bohemian family. They've set up what Ryan says is 'almost' a proper recording studio in the garage for band practice. Blood Sweat and Beers. Ruby hopes no one brings beers. If they do she trusts Ryan to say no, as he's driving home. She really does.

Lola will keep him safe. Ruby pictures Ryan driving home along the country lanes. They bought the Corolla when he was just a baby; when they got rid of the old van they'd raced about in, even camped in the back of. Lola was their first new car and they kitted her out with the best baby seat on the market. She's kept them all safe, all this time, and with over a hundred thousand miles on the clock, she's still going strong. She'll keep him safe. Ruby thinks she really will.

She gets up with a sigh and goes out along the landing to her bedroom door where she stops to listen. The house is silent apart from the sound of Paul's sleeping breath. She doesn't go in. She knows she won't sleep and will have to put the bedside light on to read and she doesn't want to disturb him. She knows she should go to bed. She'll suffer for it at work tomorrow.

I'll just go and get a glass of water, she thinks. But, down in the kitchen she sits at the table, looking at the phone on the counter. Next to it is a pot of pens and scissors; a funny little clay pot with a wonky heart on it that Ryan made for her in his last year at primary school. Ruby's thoughts are skittering all over the place but she takes an emery board from the pot and tries to concentrate on doing her nails. Insanely she looks at the emery board and thinks of all those little brown strips of cardboard, rolling along a conveyor belt in some factory being coated with powdered glass. Unbidden, an image of a scatter of broken glass on tarmac comes into her mind.

Perhaps he's decided to stay over. No he would call. He said he'd be back by eleven at the latest. It's now eleven fifteen. Maybe Thomas's mum wouldn't mind if she rang to check that he's on his way.

Then Ruby hears a car coming up the drive. It pulls up. Ruby lets out her pent up breath in a sigh of relief. She hears the crunch of feet across the gravel. Two people? She is waiting for the sound of the key in the door. It doesn't come.

Everything goes into slow motion when, instead of the sound of a key in the lock, she hears the sound of the doorknocker. Ruby gets up and moves from the kitchen through the family room into the hall. Scarcely able to breath, she walks as if she is pushing through a waist deep drift of melting snow.

One of them will be a woman, she thinks. They always send a policewoman in cases like this. More sympathetic. Will it be intensive care or the morgue? Will she take time to get dressed? Should she call Paul now or after she's opened the door? When she gets to the hospital, will Ryan be lying there, covered in wires and tubes, fighting for his life; brain damaged or maybe in a coma. Or if it's the morgue? Her baby, cold and blue - will he be lying on a slab? Or will he be burnt? Will the image of his twisted, blackened face be printed on her brain for the rest of her miserable life? She envisions Lola, steam rising from her mangled radiator, wrapped around a tree, or just a burnt out shell in a ditch.

After an eternity of torture, Ruby reaches the door. She glances through the frosted glass panel. No flashing lights – they're not in a hurry then. So it must be the morgue. No race to hold her dying son's hand – just a slow drive in heavy silence to identify the body. In the porch, two figures are backlit by the yard lights, one tall, one smaller. She cannot see their faces. She undoes the lock and opens the door with one hand, while holding onto the doorframe with the other, to prevent herself from sinking to her knees.

Ruby gets a quick kiss on the top of her head (he's taken to doing that lately) as her tall, broad, warm son pushes past her into the hallway. He places the car keys with a satisfying clatter in the bowl on the dresser and dumps his sax case down.

'Sorry to get you up Mum. Forgot my door key. Won't let it happen again.'

Ryan turns to the figure still waiting in the porch. 'Come in Harry. God, it's too cold to stand around out there! Mum, this is Harry.'

Harry doesn't look like any Harry Ruby has met before. She is small and pretty, with short dark hair and a fetchingly pierced eyebrow.

'Harry is our keyboard player, Mum. Is the spare room made up? I hope it's OK if Harry stays here tonight and gets a lift into college with me in the morning. Her car wouldn't start. Piece of old junk.'

God in Heaven! thinks Ruby, still leaning on the doorframe. Something else for me to worry about.

The Yeovil Literary Prize

2013 Highly Commended

Christopher Holt *The Flags of Our Empire*	119
Louise Warren *Cell Death*	123
Eve Bonham *I Spy With My Little Eye*	124
David Grubb *Emily Dickenson's Joke Book*	128
Tracey Iceton *Dinner for One*	129
Catherine Chanter *Photograph of a Little Girl, Bristol 1960*	134
Chris Allen *Attack of the Apache*	135
Emma Seaman *Roses All the Way*	140
David Punter *Riau Archipelago*	146
Dennis Harkness *Early Retirement*	147

THE FLAGS OF OUR EMPIRE *by Christopher Holt*

Empire Day 1946. In the great Southern Dominion, two children are dawdling home from school along a hot road of gravel. William is nine, his sister, Emily, two years younger.

The children are having a half-holiday in celebration of an Empire that will be gone by the time they reach their twenties. Emily is bringing home her Empire cards meticulously copied in coloured pencil.

William is proud of his sister. It was Emily who was chosen to plant the Empire tree, a slim wand of silky oak intended to become a blossoming landmark which they would see when they were grown up. It was the latest in an avenue of steadily towering trees going back to the reign of George the Fifth.

***

The little bush school has fourteen pupils all taught by Miss Hudson, the only teacher they have ever known. All that week, the school had been festooned in red, white and blue bunting, for Miss Hudson had a fervent loyalty to a Britain which she had never seen nor was never likely to, and an Empire she could only imagine from newsreels, picture books and the wireless.

The previous night alone in the school house, Miss Hudson had prepared for Empire Day by cutting out hundreds of little rectangles of white card just as she had done for the past thirty four years.

The class had spent the whole morning on these cards. A big chart had hung over the blackboard from which the children copied with coloured pencils, the flags of every British dominion, protectorate, mandated territory and colony throughout the world.

When they had finished, Miss Hudson looped the tiny flags together with rubber bands in neat wads, a complete set for each pupil to take home.

Before dismissal, she took the class outside on the parched grass for the Empire Day ceremony. She lined the children up smartly and told them to remove their hats. At this point a red headed girl stepped forwarded to recite Rupert Brooke's "Home Thoughts from Abroad".

After this, Miss Hudson raised her hands like a conductor and after sounding the first notes with a tuning fork, she led her little school in singing *"Land of Hope and Glory", "There'll always be an England"*

and concluding, of course, with *"God Save the King"*.

Finally Emily stepped out to the front and planted *The 1946 Tree for the Motherland*, which another girl watered from a can. Miss Hudson firmed down the soil with her flat shoes.

The sun was merciless. Miss Hudson told the pupils to give three rousing cheers for the Empire and another for the King, and after a chorused "Good afternoon, Miss Hudson", all the pupils were sent home, some on bicycles, a few on horses and others, like Emily and William, on foot.

***

The children trudge along like an elderly couple, but then everything looks old, even the road itself is rutted and worn out. The leaning, gnarled fence posts are silver grey and beyond them lone sentinels of derelict farm machinery rust among the blackberry and prickly pear, while in the barns high square Studebakers stand silent and dust bound.

This is the eighth month of drought and despite being late May, it is still a baking 98 degrees in the shade. But on the road there is no shade. Emily wears a wide bonnet, but the glare from the sun is a ubiquitous torment for her brother and forces him to adopt a habitual squint.

A giant ants' mound is a familiar landmark and when the children reach it William always says "halfway". It is not an impressive feature, just a pink swelling in the dead grass.

The boy goes over to scratch its loose surface with a stick and the furious bluish ants erupt from their tunnels, pincers wide open for battle.

"Bomb them!" he shouts, "Let 'em have it!" Ignoring the heat he races about picking up chunks of quartz which he hurls down on the nest. "Get 'em! Pi-ow! Pi-ow!" He now strafes the ants with handfuls of gravel. Fresh troops stream out in a frenzied chaos of legs and pincers. "Reinforcements needed," calls the boy, his face red. "Send in the tanks!" He finds a long piece of rusty junk by the fence and scrapes this into the mound until it looks like an open sore with the teeming ants flowing out in mass like dark blood. "Atom bombs needed! Come on, Emily, you're 'sposed to be an ally." He picks up the biggest rock he can lift and nearly overbalancing with its weight drops it squarely on the nest. "Enemy conquered," he says, his chest heaving as he slaps his dusty hands on his shorts.

All this time Emily has been keeping right back. Once as a toddler she had sat down on a nest like this and the sour smell of formic acid brought back the memory of ants trilling all over her body, the horrendous stings and her own hysterical screaming.

William's assault on the ants peters out but he now starts hunting all over the place for yet more stones. It's as if this time he wants to conceal the devastation.

Afterwards, without a word to each other, the children pick up their satchels and dawdle on once more. Behind them the nest with its covering of white stones stands out like a new grave.

They pass smaller properties whose owners run a few head of cattle and grow oranges under irrigation. Although the population was long established, none of the farmers was well off.

To avoid the sun William edges over to a clump of grey wattles set back from the road and almost blunders into a spider's web with a large curled leaf slung in the middle.

"Emily, come over here a minute. Have a look at this."

She stares very closely into the rolled leaf until she can make out a spider; its legs neatly olded up inside. "It must be shy," she whispers.

Just then they hear a car draw up, a burnished red convertible with its hood drawn back. The man behind the wheel leans over his companion and shouts across to the children. "Hey, you two, is there a shop – a local *store* around here anywhere?" His tone is clear and almost exotic. To William it is one of those city voices that you only hear on the wireless, an unconstrained echo-box convinced of its own authority.

"What are you both doing?" The voice of the young woman complements the man's perfectly. These were two of a kind, modishly dressed, their bodies folded entirely at ease in that splendid motor car.

Emily goes over to them and when the woman asks her about school, she opens her satchel. It is full of screwed up lunch paper, a bottle still containing some diluted orange juice and a kewpie doll without the stick. At last she finds the little wad of *Flags of our Empire* and as she takes off the rubber band, it snaps in her hand. The woman shuffles through the cards with a condescending smile and hands them back. Then Emily tells them about the leaf spider and both strangers look across to William.

Still crouching by the wattles, the boy holds back. He has already imbibed the poisonous notion that he and his world do not really matter very much. He leaves it to Emily to give the couple directions to the shop – less than a mile further along the road.

They drive off but within minutes the convertible is back with both occupants eating huge ice-creams. It slows down alongside, time enough for the man to call out very loudly and deliberately to the boy. "Oh by the way, did you catch the spider that caught the fly?" The children hear them laughing together as they speed away leaving the hot swirling dust to settle where it can.

Five minutes later the drought ends. A sudden clarion of magpies is lost in the cracks of thunder and the rush of a tremendous storm. A heavy driving rain rakes the wattles and lashes the road.

Emily cheers. She throws up her arms. She embraces the rain and pirouettes round and round. Her heart sings as she breathes the chilled air now scented by the sweet communion of chaste water on dry earth. On the road the quartz pebbles are washed vivid and new. William thinks about the couple in the convertible and wonders whether they had time to put the hood up.

Still spinning round and round Emily holds out her satchel at arm's length by the strap. It sails alongside her. Faster and faster, round and round – the fences, the trees, even the Great South Land itself pivots around her. And the rain teems down.

The boy stares at Emily as if seeing her for the first time. An unfamiliar tenderness wells up within him for his sister with both her plaits coming undone and her school dress soaking to the skin. She hasn't buckled the satchel properly and the *Flags of Our Empire* are all flying out, their colours running, their cardboard sodden.

He notices how clean Emily looks. She is positively shining.

And so is everything else.

CELL DEATH *by Louise Warren*

At the appointed hour a tiny hinge springs open-
and the mechanism is revealed
briefly, before dismantling itself.

This is the order of programmed death.
A cluster of chambers articulate outwards
into segments of brilliance

each one a miniature jewel in the pattern of the whole,
displayed upon the plush of internal velvet.
At the centre a seed, wrapped around a filament,

inside which the coiled up ribbon of all life
unravels, delicate as a hairspring
before blowing apart in the smallest of explosions.

You are unaware of this, the alchemist working
in the dark. Forging a billion stars
inside an inch of skin, the tendons of your heart.

I SPY WITH MY LITTLE EYE *by Eve Bonham*

The day his mother fell down the well, Henry was in the conker tree spying on their neighbour. He focussed his telescope on the old man who had just dug a hole near the fence and was moving slowly down his garden path, carrying a large black bag.

Hearing a door bang, he swivelled round to watch his mother who had come out into the yard. Wearing a yellow cardigan and carrying a large basket of wet laundry, she started to hang up the washing.

He turned back to continue his surveillance of Mr Matlock through the telescope. His parents had said he was deaf but Henry thought this was a clever pretence. He suspected that stolen goods were being buried and wanted to unmask the criminal. He planned to dial 999 and summon the police when he had the evidence.

His father had given him the telescope for his birthday, shortly after they moved to the cottage, but he found watching the countryside more exciting than stargazing. He'd taken to looking at the spiders in the barn where their dusty cobwebs hung in folds.

There was a quick flash of yellow to the right of his vision and he glanced across to the yard. The washing was blowing innocently in the breeze and there was a red object in the background, which he identified as a tractor moving along a distant field.

Henry thought his new home in the country was fabulous - what he hoped heaven would be like - with lots of open space, tractors, animals, insects - and very few people. And no-one to snigger about his name, his glasses or his freckles. His classmates teased him about his insect collection and when he brought a Sexton beetle in a jar into school, they called him 'weird'. Now he kept quiet about his discoveries. He didn't even tell them about the secret well.

A few days ago his dad was lifting some broken flagstones in the yard and had found a well underneath. Using a plumb line, they discovered it was 13 feet down to the water which was 10 feet deep. His dad had temporarily covered the dangerous hole with a large sheet of wood and forbidden his son to move it. But that evening Henry had pushed the wood partially aside to shine a torch down to the glinting water. Deciding to do an experiment, he went across to where he kept his pets and extracted his toad. He wanted to see if it could swim as well as a frog and dropped it in. There was a satisfying plop as it hit the inky water but it then disappeared. At that point his mother had called him to tea and he had dashed indoors.

Henry continued with his surveillance, wondering idly where the old man's grey dog was. Rover was almost as ancient and smelly as his master and they usually tottered about the garden together. Bored by lack of action, the boy put down the telescope and became aware of various sounds – the wind in the tree, birdsong, the distant noise of the tractor - and something high-pitched. Looking down, he saw the piece of wood covering the well and noticed the black aperture to one side. He had forgotten to pull it back over the hole the night before! Perhaps Rover had fallen in and was whining to be pulled out.

Then his brain did a somersault. His mum had disappeared from view and it was her shrieking that he could hear. He gasped in horror, scrambled down the tree and ran across.

"Mum, I'm here." Henry spied her thrashing around in the evil black water below.

"Henry, thank God. I thought you'd never hear me," His mother was treading water, looking up with a pale scared face. "Go for help. But first get me something to hold onto - the sides are too smooth."

"Is it cold?" the boy asked anxiously.

"It's freezing."

Henry looked around desperately. A few yards away lay his new football, inflated with air. He grabbed it dropped it down the shaft. "Hold onto this."

"Good boy." She said, clutching it. "Now call for help. Use my mobile – in my bag."

Indoors Henry found the mobile didn't work. His mum always forgot to re-charge it and they had no land line yet. He ran back, skidding on the stones as he braked.

"It doesn't work, Mum. I'll have to go for help."

"Don't leave me, Henry." She needed him. He must save her! Reeling from the responsibility, he had an idea. "I'm going to get Mr Matlock to help. I won't be long." There was a wail of protest from below but Henry sped off.

The old man was not pleased to see the nosy boy from next door tearing down the garden path waving his arms.

"Please come," Henry shouted. "Mum's fallen down a well." This was greeted with a blank stare. "We need help," pleaded Henry tugging on his arm. Noticing tears on his wizened face the boy saw the dog lying on the muddy path – dead. The man was burying his pet and he really was deaf! Henry spun round and tore back to the well.

"Mummy, Mr Matlock can't come."

"Find a rope, Henry. I'm getting tired and I can hold onto it while you go for help." She was trying hard not to panic.

Henry dashed into the workshop but there was no rope. Emerging into the sunlight, he thought of his mother in that dark hole and felt helpless. A huge sob burst out of him. What did his dad always say? "Use your eyes, lad."

Henry took a deep breath and, turning slowly in a circle, he missed the washing line but saw the chestnut tree and his swing. A thick strong rope! Scanning the branch, he knew he couldn't untie it whilst holding on, and if he fell off he wouldn't be able to save Mum. He needed to cut it off.

"Got an idea," he called dashing into the kitchen and grabbing a sharp knife. Holding it between his teeth like a pirate climbing rigging, he shinned up the tree and edged along the branch to the rope. Holding on with one hand, it took few minutes to hack through the thick strands so he kept calling out, "Nearly there, Mummy." To reassure her – and himself.

The rope dropped heavily to the ground and, jettisoning the knife, Henry slid down the trunk, grazing himself badly. Ignoring the searing pain, he staggered across with the heavy rope in his arms, praying it would be long enough.

"Got it, Mummy."

"Hurry, darling. I'm getting cold." He was shocked by the fear in her voice.

He looked round frantically for something to tie it round. "Where are you, Henry?" His mother sounded desperate.

He almost panicked but, taking a calming breath, he called down, "It's alright. I'm here. Just working out what to attach the rope to."

Leaning against the workshop wall were some of his Dad's wooden tree stakes and he carried one across, tied the rope round the pole and balanced it across the aperture. Then he pushed the coils over the edge. He watched as it fell down, the large knot at the bottom narrowly missing his mother as she bobbed about holding onto the football. What luck, the knot was just on the surface!

"Now, Mummy, pull yourself up to sit on the knot," he instructed her. "Wrap your legs round it like I do on the swing. That's right." Kneeling on the edge, Henry felt in control. His mother gripped the rope and heaved herself up onto the knot by kicking with her legs. Suddenly she was there, sitting with only her legs in the water. "Well done, Mummy." He felt proud of her and himself. He'd done it!

"Henry, you're amazing. I'm safe for the moment." The hope in her voice was simply wonderful. "Now go for help."

"I can see someone on a tractor. Sure you're OK?"

"Yes. Go."

So he took off across the fields remembering he'd seen a man in the lane driving a tractor and talking on his mobile. It was disappointing that he wouldn't be making the 999 call.

His Dad arrived back just after the Fire Brigade had lifted his mum out of the well and wrapped her in an emergency blanket. A reporter from the local paper turned up an hour later, keen to get the story of a local drama. He told Henry's parents that their boy had kept his cool in a crisis and was a hero.

Waiting for the school bus next day, Henry examined the impressive graze on his leg, wondering if he could bear to keep quiet about saving his mother's life until the newspaper came out on Thursday. The bus came and he climbed aboard with an exaggerated limp and more than a hint of a swagger. At school it was clear the news had leaked out.

There was no sniggering. It was the best day of his life.

He thought he might bring his telescope into school to show it to his classmates.

His favourite uncle, who was an airline pilot, always called him Harry. He might ask his new friends to do the same.

EMILY DICKENSON'S JOKE BOOK *by David Grubb*

In the upstairs room
where snow could be seen but not heard,
where downstairs voices stopped at the front door,
where the window watched for tricks of light,
Emily also worked on her Book Of Jokes;
about answers without questions,
about the way words made silences,
about the variations of impulse,
about the arrival of strangers,
about where an idea went when one didn't use it,
about the determination of the garden,
about visitors from England,
about the music in dreams;
about what other people said that she meant
in some poems that appeared to have a voice
of their own;
about how errors often corrected conformities,
about the seconds when an afternoon becomes evening,
about how we can seldom tell who we will never meet again,
about the way we dress for dances and deaths,
about what is lost between stopping and starting a clock;
about how we all go into the sky to die.

DINNER FOR ONE *by Tracey Iceton*

He's waiting to take my order. There's plenty of choice. I can have almost anything. Almost.

"Have you decided yet?" he asks.

I rake over the possibilities; steak and chips, pepperoni pizza, chicken chow mien... Then dessert; waffles and syrup, apple pie, chocolate ice-cream... I'd eat the whole damn lot if I could. Excepting the ice-cream.

Saturday afternoon. Barney took me to the park. Got us ice-creams from the concession stand. Giant cones filled with freezing clouds. Barney liked pistachio. I plumped for vanilla. Not chocolate. It was a talking point.

"Why don't you like chocolate?" Barney asked as we strolled over to a bench.

"My daddy used to bring home chocolate ice-cream, right after he'd beaten my momma to within and inch of her life. He'd say sorry, promise Jesus he'd change then we'd have to eat the ice-cream."

We sat ourselves down. The wood was warm through my worn jeans, hot where the rip in the right leg left my skin pressed bare on the cedar. Barney sat himself at one end; me at the other. A whole empty seat between us gaping like a mouth asking a question.

"You never say much about your daddy. Why's that?"

"Because I hate him. Because he's a bastard."

"Mary Lou! You're not to use language like that."

"Who cares?"

"If you go back to the Centre cussing like that Mrs Declan'll blame me."

I licked my ice-cream. It was starting to dribble down the cone, making for my hand. I raced the sugary droplets, cutting off their advance with my tongue.

"Anyways," Barney continued, "Your daddy's not like that now. He's reformed, found God. He wants to see you. He rang Mrs Declan to...."

The ice-cream was a back-handed sugar high in return for my co-operation.

"I'm not seeing him. You can't make me." I jumped up. Scooped the icy ball off the cone and pitched it at him. It struck Barney square on the chest then plopped right into his lap. He just stayed sitting there, the ice-cream all running to a sticky pool in his crotch. I ran off like I was always doing when things didn't go my way. Guess I knew right enough though, by the fact that Barney didn't chase me, that it was a done deal, my daddy coming back. Screw you, God.

At first it was supervised visits. My daddy'd show up looking all slick and polished, like he'd been to the car wash, had himself waxed up good and proper. We'd sit in the rec room with Mrs Delcan in the corner, watching us over her needlepoint or Barney keeping his eyes on one of them books he liked reading but with his ears turned our way. *Call of the Wild* was one; sometimes he'd read it to me. And my daddy sure done a good job letting them all think he was a changed man. He'd talk all nice, saying he was sorry to hear about Momma going to Jesus (like it wasn't his fault her kidneys packed in, all them times he'd kicked her about), asking how I was doing in school, offering to bring me things: wanting to pray with me, save me from sinning. But I knew it was coming. I was ready for it.

Another Saturday afternoon. More milk-and-sugar bribery and corruption.
"How's the raspberry ripple, Mary Lou?"
"Pretty good."
"Mrs Declan wants me to talk to you about something."
I'd already licked the ice-cream all the way down inside the cone. I up-ended it now. Nibbled at the bottom and started sucking like a big old pump on an engine.
"She was telling me your daddy's asking the judge about the two of you having more time together, maybes going on trips."
A lump of squishy raspberry ripple flung itself into my mouth. Hit the back of my throat with a whump. I swallowed it down in one.
"That gonna happen?"
"If you want it to."
"So I can say no, if I don't want it to?"
"You can say no, Mary Lou, but you gotta think about the future. What're you gonna do when you've turned sixteen? When's your birthday again?"
"December."
"If you get yourself back on good terms with your daddy the two of you can live together. Where else're you gonna go when you're too old to stay at the Centre?"
I started thinking then, 'bout it all. Planning. Barney was right. I was needing to find me somewheres other than the damn Children's Centre. Somewheres they weren't never gonna kick me out. I munched up the cone, my crunchy teeth-marks meeting in the middle.
"Alright, fine. Whatever."

My daddy took me out to the lake he'd taken us all to before, on them times when he had money in his pocket and visions of happy family living in his liquor-soaked brain.

It was darkish when we got there but I'd've recognised the cabin in the pitch black. As we drove up to it in the dented, clunking, juddering Ford he'd acquired I was thinking how quiet the old place was, the land all dowsed in purple as the night came up behind us and no sign of anybody. Just the two of us. Times before, when it was the three of us, the whole damn lake basin filled up with them two bawling at each other then the thuds of his fists pounding into my momma's saggy fleshfolds and her yelling blue murder at him.

The cabin was cold, that bone cold of a place unlived-in. It smelled all fusty too, like a racoon had up and died and was rotting away to dry, brittle fur in some dark corner. He carried the bags. I followed, sniffing the air around me. The call of the wild was out there in them woods. And it was coming on me.

"You know how to make a pot of coffee?" he asked, dumping our bags on the grey, flaky floorboards.

"Course, I'm not dumb."

"Well, stove's there," he jabbed through the frozen air with his thumb, "I'll see 'bout chopping some wood."

I left him to it. Whack whack whack. He pounded that old axe with a neat rhythm, keeping time better than a drummer boy. Just like how he used to hit on my momma. Whack whack whack.

When the coffee was made I took him a cup. The last of the light was leaving. He had his sleeves rolled up, meaning his business, and a cigarette dangling. His baby Jesus tattoo was smirking at me.

"You got another of those?" I pointed at the glowing ember wedged in the crack of his tight mouth.

"You oughtn't to be smoking."

"Says who?"

He gave me the cigarette. We stood there, getting darker and darker, smoking and sipping our coffee.

"God's country. Your momma sure did like it out here," he said with a sigh, "Still, she's with the Lord, now."

"I'm getting cold," I said and went back inside.

He stomped in a few paces behind me, his arms filled with hunks of wood he'd hacked up with his own bare strength. Strength that ran in my veins.

"See if you can get that going. I'll fix us some supper."

Poor Momma, she'd've upped and right to it, most times anyways. I let him go over to the cupboards and root through two before I stirred myself. There was a box of matches, some firelighters. I lifted the poker. It was heavy and cold in my hand, left a sooty stain on my palm. I wiped my hand off on the rug. Black grime smeared itself east to west. I prodded about amongst the logs with the pointy end, stabbing and jabbing, killing the lumps of wood that wouldn't burn. I beat on that fire 'til it submitted. Flames coughed into life at my hand.

"There's not much here. Tins of stuff that'll probably be alright," he called out, "some peanut butter. Damn stuff never goes bad."

"I don't want peanut butter."

"Pork and beans it is."

He heated them up in a grubby pan. Said grace, head all bowed nice and proper. Licked his plate clean. I chewed slow and careful, kept finding myself grinding down on shifty bits of grit. I only ate half what he set in front of me.

"Waste's sinful, Mary Lou."

I shrugged so he helped himself. I watched him wolf down his supper, gobbling pork and beans like he was a starving man and that was the finest plate of eats he'd ever been given. The tin bowl rang out as he dropped it on the stone hearth.

"Thank you, Lord," he said, patting his full-to-busting belly. He rested some, well-pleased with his lot, "I brung you a treat, Mary Lou." He lumbered to where the bags were and rustled through them. Straightened up with a tub in his hand. "Might be a bit melted but it'll still go down nice, I reckon. Chocolate's your favourite, right?"

He fetched two spoons. Came to sit next to me on the flattened-out couch. No space between us, just me and him, side by side, two birds on a wire: sitting ducks.

"Dig in, Mary Lou."

The browness in the tub was all sloppy, a gloppy, sludgy mess of cocoa and cream, turning sour in my lap. He stuck the two spoons into the mush, spearing them down into the sweet heart. Dug one back out, bringing it to his mouth laden with gooey stuff the colour of puke. Cleaned the whole of it off with his lips and tongue. Smacked with satisfaction and tossed the spoon on the floor. Then he shuffled on his ass so he was facing side on to me. I felt his hand on the back of my neck. It was sweaty and warm. Sticky.

"You were always a good girl, Mary Lou. I'm sure sorry it's been such a time since we seen each other. But, Lord be praised, I've got you back and right glad I am."

His hand was resting on my shoulder now, the fingers twitching the cotton of my t-shirt, crawling their sweet way down towards my titties.

"You're pretty, just like your momma." He leaned over. The couch dipped in the middle, tipping me over to him. His breath was all spicy beans and pork in my ear. His lips were tacky when he planted them on my cheek. "Your momma's gone, but I still got you, don't I, sugar?"

He took hold of my chin. Twisted my jaw round 'til we were eyeballing each other, predator and prey, getting ready to mate with each other. He kissed my mouth. I tasted his pork and beans. That one spoonful of chocolate ice-cream. The spoon was still lying on the hearth. Right alongside the poker. I made my mind up. Grabbed me a weapon.

He's still waiting for me to order.

"Hey, Jackson, I haven't got all day. You want something to eat or not?" He clangs his baton up and back over the bars.

"Yeah, but I don't want nothing off this menu. Can I get some peanut butter sandwiches?"

He raises his eyebrows. "That's what you want? Peanut butter sandwiches? You want jelly on those too?"

"Nope, just peanut butter and get it on there good and thick."

He shrugs. "Suit yourself, Jackson. What a last supper that's gonna make."

"Better than old pork and beans, melted chocolate ice-cream," I reply.

He shakes his head. "Guess they're right about you, you really are nuts!"

I watch his khaki back as he strides down the corridor. When he's out of sight I perch on my bunk. I'm looking forward to it. I haven't had peanut butter since I was five. Since the doc said it could kill me if I ate enough. Them that wants to see me to fry for killing my daddy'll be mighty disappointed in the morning.

PHOTOGRAPH OF A LITTLE GIRL, BRISTOL, 1960 *by Catherine Chanter*

The little girl is lit from behind by a circular window.
These portholes transformed the suburban houses
in this city of slaves into ocean liners, whose owners
trimmed their sails for Ireland, where trade in commodities
was brisk as the westerlies, where seeded and ripened
and numbered by nuns, lay the home market babies.

To the left of the little girl, a few Christmas roses,
in keeping with the rural theme and hand embroidered lace,
the daisies in the smocking and the spotless cotton
of the party dress, and oh! the cleanliness, the godliness,
the whiteness of her unsmiling face; her ill conceived
beginnings soft focused from the picture and forgotten.

The little girl holds her favourite toy and the photographer
is pleased with the contrasts and similarities,
the way its white eyes stare like moons and hers
pool black at him, the way both smiles are stitched.
How well conceived this study in black and white photography,
the picture of the two of us, my gollywog and me.

ATTACK OF THE APACHE *by Chris Allen*

Jack Gillespie – hypnotherapist and expert on the paranormal – was seated in the studio at his home on the All Saints Road in the Clifton area of Bristol. It was his last consultation of the day on Friday 25th Oct 2013 and he was deeply puzzled. The session was with a new client – a young Scot; it was turning out to be a very unusual case ... Jack needed to find out more.

"So how long have you been having this dream, Angus?"

"Nearly two months; it started at the beginning of September. I have it every Thursday night, that's when I stay overnight in Yeovil at a guest house on Hendford Hill ... but not at any other time of the week for some reason. The same thing happens every time; I'm driving home on Friday afternoon along the A37 towards Bristol when I see an Apache attack helicopter flying low directly ahead of me."

Jack nodded. "Then you hear a bang and you see smoke and flames come out of its engines."

"Aye, then the aircraft goes into a tailspin; the pilot manages to pull the nose up somehow but the Apache veers out of control and heads straight back along the road towards my car and ... there's a head on collision. I always wake up in a cold sweat, scared shitless. I've stopped using the A37 to drive home; I cut across country using the A303 and the A358 to pick the motorway. It's quite a long detour but I feel safer. I haven't spoken to anybody else about this; I'm beginning to wonder if I'm losing it – perhaps I've been on this contract with Westland for too long. It's been nearly eight years; I started back in 2006."

"And you've always worked on the Apache; have you?"

"Aye, that's right, on – HUMS – the Health Usage and Monitoring System; it's intended to reduce running costs by optimising the maintenance schedule. The major components on the Apache are hellishly expensive; you don't want to replace them in a hurry. Bear in mind that each helicopter costs about 60 million quid and it won't come as a surprise if I say that the MoD may scrap the whole fleet by 2017 or, at the very least, reduce the size of it. I'll be as sick as a parrot if that happens; I've worked on the programme for so long."

Angus paused for a moment before continuing. His accent sounded a little diluted to Jack's ear; his tone was – middle class – well educated, he made little use of Scottish slang.

"By the way, there's something about my dream I should have mentioned before."

"What's that?"

"The helicopter's got 700 written in large white numbers along the fuselage; the numbers are clearly visible"

"What's so unusual about that?"

Angus sighed. "Well, 67 Apaches were ordered originally for the Army Air Corps; the allocated tail numbers are in the range ZJ166 to ZJ233. 700 isn't a valid number; I don't understand."

"Angus, that's because you're taking the dream too literally. It's a product of your unconscious; its language is often very symbolic and metaphorical. It works in a different way to your everyday conversational mind. Once you understand that, it's sometimes possible to tease out the hidden message... if there is one. But bear in mind that not all dreams are meaningful – very far from it. Sometimes, these recurrent dreams are triggered by stress or unusual difficulties in your life. Is there anything like that happening to you right now?"

Jack waited; he could tell from the pained expression on his client's face that he had touched a nerve.

He knew from long experience that people – particularly men – are often loath to speak about anything of a personal nature, especially if it reveals vulnerability or weakness.

Jack took a moment to look at the young man seated opposite on a black leather recliner chair and reflected on what he already knew about his client from earlier conversation. Angus Buchanan was in his mid-thirties, handsome in a rugged sort of way with dark hair – cut short; he was of average height – about 5'8" and stocky – about 14 stone. He was dressed for warmth and comfort: jeans, trainers, casual shirt and a thick jumper.

He's got the build of a rugby scrum-half – thought Jack; this impression was reinforced when Angus opened his mouth to speak, revealing a missing lower incisor tooth. Born and raised in Edinburgh, Angus was an only child; his parents were well off professional people. Angus went to Bristol University where he graduated with a degree in Computer Software Engineering. Jack wondered about that – why incur the tuition fees? Why not study in Scotland?

"I'm getting divorced; it's final at the end of the month. I'm pretty gutted." Angus was choking with emotion – having difficulty getting the words out. "It's only now coming home to me; I suppose I've been hoping that I might get back together with Pat even at this late stage – how sad is that?"

"How long have you been married?"

"Quite a while, we met as undergraduates; she's a local girl. We set up home in Bristol. I worked for BAE Systems in Filton for a few years and then went contracting. She's an estate agent. We've both done quite well for ourselves; we bought a decent property just up the road about three years ago. It's up for sale now; I moved out last year. I'm renting a flat in Kingsdown."

"Any kids?"

"No, that was part of the problem; I wanted some bairns but Patricia was more into her career. She met some guy – a manager – at work and they started an affair. I didn't catch on until too late. I confronted the big Jessie; it turned nasty and I cleaned his clock. Pat was pissed at that; she put a restraining order on me."

"Did you lose your tooth in the fight?"

Angus smiled. "Ach no, that was from playing five a side at work a few months ago; it got a bit out of hand. I haven't got around to getting my mouth fixed."

Angus looked into the middle distance before continuing.

"I guess Pat and I were bound to break up. She's a couple of inches taller; she towers over me in high heels. I suppose we've always looked a bit ridiculous together. Ach, it's a bugger how these petty things can end up ruining your life."

Acting on a sudden hunch and without preamble Jack asked: "Has this time of year got any special significance to you?"

Angus broke eye contact; for a moment, Jack could have sworn that his client was close to tears. A minute or so passed before Angus replied.

"I lost both of my parents in a car crash in October 1997 when I was 17. I lived with my uncle for a while but I had to get away from Edinburgh – leave Scotland. That's why I opted to go to Bristol University; I inherited a fair bit so money wasn't a problem.

Jack nodded in understanding.

"Angus, there's a pattern beginning to emerge here ... Have you, by any chance, spoken to anybody at work recently about the possibility of an Apache helicopter crashing?"

Angus was surprised. "Aye, the month before last – I think it was – my boss was telling me about how close they came to disaster at the Flight Shed in Yeovil."

"What happened?"

"Well, the maintenance crew were prepping an Apache for a test flight. A very experienced guy thought there was something odd about the engine noise even though he was wearing ear defenders. He insisted that the operation had to be cancelled and that the aircraft should be stripped down and checked over. This was a gutsy call to make because the clock's running under those circumstances and the costs of delaying a test flight are prohibitive. Anyway, they took the helicopter apart and initially couldn't find anything. However, when they came to have a closer look, they found a very unusual hairline fracture in the Main Rotor Gear Box which might have resulted in catastrophic failure at any time."

Angus looked bemused. "Why is this relevant?"

"Angus, I think the dream you've been having is just a metaphor; it's a reaction to the stress of having to endure divorce proceedings exacerbated by memory of the death of your parents due to the time of year. Your unconscious has created this recurrent fantasy because you're in a personal tail spin and booked for a crash landing when your marriage finally comes to an end. And that conversation with your boss probably acted as trigger. Am I correct in thinking that the dream first started shortly after you were told about the incident in the Flight Shed?"

Angus thought for a moment before replying.

"Aye, that's right, a few days after; this is beginning to make some sense. That's a relief; I was beginning to think I was going bloody daft. So, you don't think that the dream is predictive in anyway?"

"I can't be certain, Angus, but I think it's unlikely. You should find that the dream goes away now that you have an insight into its possible significance. Look, why don't you come back at this time next week? You're facing another difficult period in your life; a hypnotic session to boost your self-esteem and confidence might help you cope better."

Angus readily agreed; Jack made out an appointment card and gave it to his client.

The following Friday – 1st Nov 2013 – Jack received the following e-mail from Angus just before midday.

"Hi Jack,

I didn't have the dream again last night. What a relief! I slept well for the first time in ages. I've decided to go home on the A37 this afternoon just to put the whole matter to rest. I'll see you at 8 o'clock as arranged.

Best Regards, Angus"

Jack was pleased but thought no more about it; he got on with the rest of his day.

At around 6 PM, Jack went out for a run down towards the Clifton Suspension Bridge. He returned home about half an hour later; his wife – Jill – called down to him as he came through the front door.

"Jack, can you call the Avon and Somerset police and ask for Sergeant Saunders? I left his number on the pad by the phone in the hall."

Intrigued, Jack did so; his call was picked up almost immediately: *"Sergeant Saunders speaking."*

"Hello there, this is Jack Gillespie; my wife told me that you rang earlier."

"Oh yes, Mr Gillespie; thank you for calling back. Do you happen to know someone by the name of Angus Buchanan?"

"Yes, as a matter of fact, I do; he's a client, I'm expecting him to show up here later on this evening."

There was a short but quite definite pause before the policeman continued.

"I'm afraid not, sir. Mr Buchanan was involved in a fatal accident this afternoon on the A37. I was in attendance; he was pronounced dead at the scene. We've been trying to contact his next of kin. I found your appointment card in his wallet."

Jack felt like throwing up. "What happened?" he gasped.

"I regret to say that Mr Buchanan's vehicle was in head on collision with a very large motorhome which veered out of control and went over to his side of the road. It was one of the new model Apaches; he didn't stand a chance. The driver of the motorhome was shaken but only slightly injured as were the other occupants. However, he failed the breathalyser; he was arrested and has been charged. I'm afraid it was a case of excessive lunch time drinking – all too commonplace these days."

Jack was stunned, sick and off balance. "What type of motorhome did you say?"

"Let me check my notes, sir ... O yes, it was a new 2013 Auto-trail Apache 700."

ROSES ALL THE WAY *by Emma Seaman*

I don't know how I managed to lose Rob at the train station, but now here I am, all alone in this achingly romantic garden, and it is so warm, and my head hurts and honestly, it is just so like him - like our whole relationship. We always seem to be just missing each other, misunderstanding each other.

I used to joke with my friends about Rob's quaint British obsession with gardens.

'If we ever get married,' I'd declare, 'he'll surely insist that we honeymoon at Kew.' But it doesn't seem so funny, not any more. I had such high hopes for our day in this fairytale garden; tucked in the rolling countryside like a vintage jewel on green velvet, the castle's twin rose-red towers soar above the paintbox flowerbeds like giant, perfectly pointed pencils. It is all so storybook, so sweet and unexpected and faintly absurd, that I half-expect to see Rapunzel leaning out of the top window to let down her hair.

I wonder if I should locate the tea-room, and wait for Rob there. I am acquiring a decidedly English taste for cuppas; indeed, I am feeling increasingly distant from my old New York, workaday self, that sharp-suited graphic designer cab-dashing between clients. Recently, I've noticed that all my illustrations are miraculously blooming with bright flowers and twirling, curling vines, as if Rob's gardens are stealthily colouring every part of my life.

'The countryside isn't the back of beyond anymore,' he reassures me, 'If we relocate, you can still work via email, express up to London whenever you need. And just think what we can make together there; a home, our own little corner of paradise, and who knows,' he looks away shyly at this point, 'maybe even a family.'

I wander onwards, through a nut-tree grove where drifts of snowdrops sway delicately round my ankles. I fancy that if I listen closely enough, I will hear them ringing a silvery peal; but no, the cooing of ring-doves is the only sound, for as I drift deeper into the heart of the garden, the crowds have simply melted away. I expected it to be busier than this, for the station platform was liberally sown with happily chattering ladies in sensible footwear, their Cath Kidston rucksacks bulging with flasks of tea and packets of sandwiches, botanical notebooks brandished at the ready.

The snowdrops eventually give way to bluebells, lapping the path like pools of shady water, and then the way narrows into a close little alley of looming dark hedges. Just when I think I can't stand the gloom any longer, the garden opens out before me again, flooded with light. I am surrounded by colour and scent: creamy vanilla from the palest-yellow clematis scrambling in profusion along the walls; the savoury salt-breeze tang of thyme, its tiny purple buds abuzz with fat bees, and strongest of all, the heady opulent perfume of a thousand roses.

On the worn brick steps in front of me sit an elderly couple, instructing a young man in shirtsleeves. As I approach he touches one hand deferentially to his brow and pushes a laden wheelbarrow down the gravelled path and away out of view. Now I know that I have really wandered off the beaten track; I didn't realise there were people living here, like exhibits in a museum. Sometimes it seems there's so much history in this country that it bursts through at the seams - you can turn a corner and stumble upon it at any moment.

'Are you one of the Shillingses?' the lady says, giving me a swift up-and-down, 'No, p'raps not. You don't have quite the look.'

Her voice is imperious, but her face droops in charming, rather mournful lines; her huge soulful eyes as chocolaty-dark as the Alsatian resting his grizzled head on her lap. She toys with the thick ruff of fur at the animal's throat, tugging it gently with her elegant, worn fingers, weighted with tarnished silver rings.

'Shillingses?' I reply politely, 'I'm not related to anyone of that name; I'm Laurie Firbank.'

'Oh, one of our American cousins, I should have guessed,' the woman says with a little roll of her eyes at her companion. 'Still, I do like your frock, quite divine. And those painted toenails; look Hadji, how very daring!'

If the woman, or rather *lady*, looks rather boho in her burnt-orange silk shirt and sturdy boots laced to the knee, then 'dapper' is the only word I can apply to her husband. He is so very unexpected in this rustic setting, with his chalk-stripe suit, plump ruddy face and neatly clipped moustache above a small, rather sensuous mouth. He puffs at a briar pipe, and the burned-paper smoke of the tobacco wreathes amongst the rose trees like summer mist.

'*Shillingses* is our pet-name for paying visitors,' he informs me kindly. 'Have you enjoyed your shilling's worth so far?'

'I saw snowdrops,' I say, then realise how dumb that sounds on such a very hot day.

'Ah, so you discovered my famous Nuttery,' he smiles.

'We know all know about that, dear,' the lady interjects, 'Now Hadji, move over, do; let the poor gel sit down.'

I hesitate, then gather my skirt round my knees, sinking gratefully onto the bottom step next to her.

'The scent of all these roses *is* making me feel light-headed,' I say.

'You can't swoon here, most unseemly,' the lady says firmly. 'Besides, it's a nonsense; there's no such thing as a single rose note.'

She strides down the rose-walk, the old dog padding softly after her, and snips at the flowers until she's gathered an armful.

'This apricot rose should remind you of Japanese tea...' I dutifully sniff the satiny bloom thrust beneath my nose. '...while this crimson-striped beauty is utterly raspberries and cream, and this white specimen is rather reminiscent of one of Madame Chanel's perfumes.'

I nod eagerly and she sits back down beside me.

'Fabulous, aren't they?' she says proudly. 'So varied; some delicate as the brush of a butterfly's wing, while others reek as though already halfway to decay.'

Her eyes are avid, shining as if candle-lit from within, and her long fingers grasp me just above one knee.

'Vita,' her husband admonishes gently, with a little shake of his head. There is a pause, one tiny moment, and then the lady gives my knee a squeeze and takes her hand away.

'My Harold has a gimlet eye my dear; the mind of an architect with a genius for line and form. But the scent and colour – well, that is all mine. You should see my white garden in the moonlight; the moths rising like ghosts and the irises simply glowing... the absence of any hue bestows an even greater grandeur.'

'You are so passionate...' I say, admiringly.

'Obviously one puts so much of oneself into a garden, but then nature takes its course, changing with every season. Sometimes I fear this garden is growing its own sweet way, despite my best efforts,' the lady sighs.

Her husband looks at her queerly, eyes narrowed against his curling pipe-smoke,

'You're all out of kilter Vita... it's probably the heat.'

Then he smiles at me.

'Now, tell me my dear; why were you wandering so wan and lonely?'

'I'm supposed to be meeting my partner,' I say haltingly. Then somehow, the words tumble out of me, about Rob and the ruin he wants to rebuild, to transform into our own Eden. I can handle any difficult client with charm, but am helpless in the face of that old house, all woodworm and crumbling plaster, wallpaper hanging in shreds like sloughed-off skin. And the garden? It's a tangled welter of thorns and weeds; brambles high as my head, bindweed trumpeting defiance. I blush, realise I'm rambling, and say, 'It's just that because Rob and I are so different, I worry we'll split.'

'Good Lord; whoever planted that notion in your head?' The gentleman exclaims, 'Difference is the absolute key to marriage, like oysters and pearls, snowdrops and roses…'

I sigh. Oh Rob, dear Rob, where have you gone? I need you here, my horny-handed son of toil, caressing me with hands roughened from digging, yet surprisingly gentle for all that.

'Quite right, Harold! We enjoy the most unorthodox arrangements; we may look like a couple of respectable old sticks, but we'd shock you terribly if only you knew.'

I smile politely, and Lady Vita continues in a stage whisper,

'I miss Harold dreadfully when he's up in Town on business my dear, but could quite cheerfully choke him with one of his own bow-ties when he's here.'

'And I love Rob, but his life-plan scares me…'

'Don't be so lily-livered! You should have seen this place when I first found it. We quite fell in love with the old wreck – even though the garden was a wilderness of abandoned bedsprings and rusting sardine tins; acres of cabbage allotments where my precious roses now bloom. You must simply hire plenty of staff my dear, then keep them away from the cider.'

'Rob's place is not quite on this scale,' I murmur.

'How could it be?' The lady looks down her elegant, greyhound-slender nose, 'One can sense the history here, almost breathe it sometimes. I always hope to walk round a corner and see the Elizabethans, like stepping into a play.'

'That was exactly how I felt when I saw you,' I say.

'Oh, I am not quite history yet, I hope, but if these gardens should take on a little of my essence… oh I do trust so. They are quite the best thing I've ever done.'

Sir Harold nods.

'She's absolutely right, for once. And remember my dear; she that dares not grasp the thorn should never crave the rose.'

He knocks his pipe against the step and stands up, holding out a hand for his wife. She accepts his arm graciously, though she also slips me the very briefest ghost of a wink.

'Yes, we must be getting on; *tempus fugit* and all that. Come again my dear, I'm sure you will. But bring your young fellow with you next time.'

I watch them retreating across the rose garden, side-by-side and amiably bickering, the ancient dog lumbering at their heels. Maybe, if creating a garden together is what it takes to be with Rob, to grow old with him... I lean my throbbing head back against the cool stone steps. It's so very comfortable here in the sunshine, with the sun piercing through the leaves to pattern my face, my eyelids weighted with sleep. As I drift, I feel a tiny start of alarm; Rob will be waiting for me, but I really am so very drowsy, and surely Rob will understand. I must tell him, must tell him...

'Laurie! Darling, can you hear me?'

The scent of roses is even stronger now, and I open my eyes on a sea of fondant-pink blooms, full-petalled as peonies, with a citrus-tinged, almost edible scent. I smile up into Rob's face, blanched paler than one of Lady Vita's midnight flowers, the sprinkling of stubble along his jawline like ground black pepper. My head aches, oh God, how it hurts. And those roses are not growing in Lady Vita's garden, but thrust in a plastic vase, and I'm lying prone on a hard, white-sheeted bed.

'Oh Rob; I was waiting for you in the garden, I must have fallen asleep.'

My voice is oddly raspy. I try to sit up, but sway, have to lean against Rob's oak-hard arm to catch my breath.

'Laurie, we never got to the garden. You were running to catch the train, don't you remember? You caught your heel in a grating and fell. Out like a light, and I've been so very worried... You were wandering, and for a while I thought they wouldn't be able to bring you back.'

'But I saw the snowdrops under the trees, smelled those wonderful roses!'

'Oh sweetheart...' he says, a husky catch in his voice, 'Oh my poor love... I've been reading aloud while you slept – telling you all about Lady Vita and her husband, about the fabulous garden they created at Sissinghurst. I so want to take you there, show you what we could achieve together.'

He holds out a battered, much-thumbed hardback, and I turn it over in my hands.

'There they are!' I tell him, 'I met them both this afternoon; a little unusual, but mostly delightful.'

I peer at the shadowy sepia photo, then read the photo caption, the dates. They are long-gone, even though the garden they made lives on. I touch one fingertip to the faces, trace the now-familiar lines, then I see the worried frown that crosses Rob's face and put the book down.

'Roses and snowdrops together in June?' He laughs, 'Oh, Laurie, you crazy girl... but I'll make a horticulturalist of you yet.' He puts his arms around me and holds me tight.

'Oh, it'll be roses, roses all the way,' I murmur, gazing at Rob's bouquet of perfect blooms; *Fantin Latour*, pink as sun-blush, sweet as candy. I nestle my cheek against his shoulder; and as if the bouquet has been caressed by an invisible hand, a shower of rose-petals falls to the floor, silent as summer rain.

RIAU ARCHIPELAGO *by David Punter*

Black water pooling
    Silver-streaked, like haematite, like pain
Down among the mangroves silent
    Slopping and the chug of river
Boat between emerald claws,
    Dark tripods squatting in brine.

Thin palings rising
    Netted trellises where the fish
Crimsoned by night jump in arcs
    Of serpentine silhouette
Against bamboo, sea-oak, palm
    Of paradise in the sea-eagle's clutch.

Here among these unending verges
    Of bark and coral depths are plumbed
By the shadowed sailor walking
    Over the night taff-rail where
Memory laps the fishing-stakes
    With circles of ebb and wrack.

Slipping along the northerly coast of Mapur
    (Pale sand and towering casuarina)
A solid rain pebbles waves like
    Jewel-heavy greaves in ranks
Across a metal landscape, the water
    Ranged in pride above its coral secrets.

EARLY RETIREMENT *by Dennis Harkness*

Edna's favourite treat in September was the apples. Not your common-or-garden Discoveries, which were well over by then and just didn't keep. And *certainly* not the Golden so-called Delicious or the Granny Smiths that were in the shops. They were all brought in containers from Chile or Spain or wherever it was they sprayed them and waxed them and stuck gluey labels on them.

No, what she adored was picking a ripe Cox's Orange Pippin fresh from the tree in her cottage garden and eating it on the spot; or taking it to her recliner on the lawn if there was an Indian Summer, and luxuriating in the luscious flavour of the fruit's juices as she half-lay there reading the latest P D James murder mystery. Bliss! There was something to be said for an early retirement after all.

Besides, teaching had changed. When the blackboard in her classroom had been expelled in favour of the Interactive Electronic Whiteboard, Edna Coles had tried to adjust her methods to the new technology. But why should she have to? Her experience, of thirty-five years teaching lower juniors, showed in the success levels of the children in her care. She had always managed, by a mixture of threats and bribes, to get them reading and writing to the best of their varied abilities before passing them on to the next year's teacher. Even 'The Year Group of Death', so called in the staffroom because of their uniquely dreadful mixture of naughtiness and educational inadequacy, had become manageable, thanks to her efforts, by the time they moved up to the next class in the village school.

Miss Coles had striven for a whole year to adjust to the Headteacher's urgings that she should emulate her pupils' keyboard skills and make use of the enormous potential of the internet. He still seemed to think that there was insufficient 'value-added' in the achievements of her class. *Value Added? Ghastly expression! What did he know? Young whippersnapper! Thirty years old and he thought he knew more about eight-year-olds than she did. She was teaching them before he was born, for goodness sake! And children nowadays were the same as always.*

She would never forget that May afternoon when the Head stepped into her classroom. The girls and boys had gone home and she was busy pinning some of their best pictures to the wall.

"Ah, there you are, Edna!" *Where else would I be at half past four in the afternoon? Idiot! And why can't he call me Miss Coles, as Mr Armitage, my first Headmaster, used to? He showed the staff some respect.*

"Still busy, I see!"

"Of course, Mr Jones. Always something needs doing." *Try telling that to Miss Tebbitt, the flighty young teacher with Class Six next door. Off home every day at four o'clock on the dot. And does the Headteacher do anything about it? No, because all she has to do is to flutter her mascara at him and he goes weak at the knees. And in the head!*

"I believe we said we'd meet in my office. Mrs Jenkins is waiting."

"Mrs Jenkins?"

"The Union rep."

"Oh! Oh yes of course, I'd quite forgotten it was Thursday."

"Never mind, Edna," he said with that thin smile which made him look even more than usually like a constipated weasel, "Could you pop along now, do you think?" *No 'please'! And he didn't wait for an answer.*

She listened to his steel-tipped heels clipping down the corridor. Of course! The National Union of Teachers woman . He'd invited her along for the meeting. It was to discuss 'ways and means', he'd said. Ways and means to do what exactly? No doubt she was soon to find out.

She tidied the pile of pupils' artwork on her desk and tucked it away in a drawer before locking it. She gathered up the green plastic box containing children's workbooks - her marking task for that evening - and took it to her Micra in the carpark. After she'd locked the boot, she returned to the classroom. She picked up her handbag and went to the washroom. She brushed her neat bob of white hair and dabbed a touch of powder on her nose. *He can wait a bit longer. Ways and means indeed!*

"Ah, here you are," the Head said, louder than he meant to, when she finally arrived at his office, "Have a seat! This is Gwyneth." She and Edna nodded to each other. Mrs Jenkins was grey and over made-up. A dull trade union woman. Edna mentally dismissed her. *Mutton dressed as lamb? Unlike Mr Jones. Wolf in rat's clothing, more like! At this point Mr Armitage would have offered us both a cup of tea. Some hope!*

"Now then," the Head went on, "As you know, Edna, with pupil numbers declining the governors have decided that we have to cut down from six to five classes. With Gwyneth's help I've been negotiating with County, and they have, reluctantly I have to say, agreed to allow you to receive your full pension if you take early retirement."

"Early retirement? But I'm only 59!"

He scanned a form displayed on his computer screen. "Sixty next month, I believe."

"And what about young Miss Tebbitt? I understood the procedure was 'last in, first out'. Surely she should be the first to go." *Fat chance. The flirty little hussy has him wrapped right round her varnished little fingernail.*

"Other things being equal, you may be right, Edna." He glanced at Mrs Jenkins for support, but her eyes seemed to be glued to the notice board alongside him. "However, there is also a case for considering performance. And the Value-Added tables suggest that in the two years since I introduced the new computers you have found it a struggle to meet targets. I don't think you'd deny that."

Mrs Jenkins nodded her silent agreement. The die was cast. Smirking Mr Jones handed Edna a sheaf of forms for signature. And six weeks later he presented her with a bunch of flowers together with a hideous teaset bought with money collected by the staff and Parents' Association. She said a tearful farewell to the children in her class. Her career was over. Prematurely. And it was all his fault. Mr Jones. He'd be sorry.

It was the man from Shiftit who unwittingly gave her the idea. Him and Ruth Rendell. Shiftit was the company Edna telephoned when the septic tank needed emptying, which was every few years. And the week after her enforced retirement, flushing trouble suggested that the time had come round again. The driver who arrived in his shiny red tanker was new to her - and her installation new to him. "Blimey, that's a big one," he declared as he peered through the open manhole, "You could get lost in there, and no mistake!"

After he'd gone, Edna returned to her latest read, a Ruth Rendell thriller, with Inspector Wexford baffled as usual until the last chapter. A murder committed, but no corpse to be found! Aha, she guessed halfway through, the answer lies in the soil!

Her plan was simple. As she knew, during the last week of the summer holidays the Headteacher would be in school for a few hours daily to prepare for the term ahead. On the Monday afternoon Edna slipped on her gloves and took a walk through the village. Her cottage being only ten minutes from the school, she had every cause to go that way en route to the post office. Sure enough, his car was parked there. An ugly little red sporty thing, a typical bachelor man's toy. Otherwise, the school carpark was empty. Later in the week, Edna knew, the school secretary and classroom teachers would also arrive. This was the window of opportunity.

She let herself through the gate and tapped on the headteacher's window. He looked up from his desk and upon her signal came to unlock the front door.

"I am so sorry to bother you, Mr Jones."

"Edna! How are you? Enjoying retirement?" *A fat lot you care!*

"Yes, thanks to you, Mr Jones," she lied, "but I was wondering if you could spare five minutes to lend me a hand? I have a problem, and I need a man's strength to deal with it." This was not strictly true. Edna Coles was no little old lady. During her teacher training she'd been a muscular captain of the college hockey team. Mr Jones on the other hand was short and, well, weedy.

"Yes, of course!"

"It's at my house."

As they drove the short distance in his ghastly car, she kept herself low in the seat. It would not be convenient if the vicar or nosey Mrs Brazier from the W.I. noticed her just then. She guided him to park behind her garage, out of sight from the lane.

"It's my septic tank," she said as they closed the car doors, "I think it's blocked, but I can't move the manhole cover, to have a look."

"No problem!" He followed her across the lawn to where the septic tank was buried, next to her garden shed. "Is this the one?"

"That's it," she said, filled with an extraordinary calm, "I just couldn't budge the lid. I'm so glad you could come."

He crouched down to take hold of the handles on the metal cover. She noticed with surprise he had a bald patch. At his age! Miss Tebbitt wouldn't like that, she thought as, simultaneously, she reached behind the adjoining hydrangea bush where her heavy old hockey stick was concealed. She raised it high in the air and with all her strength brought it down on his unsuspecting head.

Letting out a tiny grunt he slumped on his face across the manhole. She heaved him aside and moved the heavy cover away. Her mind cool, she felt in his jacket for the car keys. Pocketing them, she also removed his wallet - if remains were found in ten years time it wouldn't do for him to be identified. Then she eased his body through the manhole. It plopped into the stinking effluent. "Bye-bye, Mr Jones," she cooed, "Enjoy your early retirement!" She slid the cover back into place.

Still wearing her gloves, she went to the house, took down from its hook in the hall her late father's old trilby and scarf. Checking first that there was nobody about in the lane, she donned the hat, wrapped the scarf round her so that her face was half hidden, and drove his car back to the school. She parked it in its normal place, stuffed hat and scarf into a carrier bag, closed the gate and reset its combination lock. Only *his* fingerprints would show up. Then she bagged her gloves before strolling on to the post office to buy stamps. Edna owed a letter to her sister in sunny Australia. Now that she was retired, perhaps she would visit her for Christmas. Or even permanently.

That thought was far from her mind a month later as she lay back in the late September sun and took another scrumptious bite from a perfect Cox's Pippin. The mystery of Mr Jones's disappearance was now old news. Much more interesting to Edna was her book. Adam Dalgliesh's latest case. The murder victim was such a bitch that nobody seemed to mind that she was dead.

Edna wondered how Miss Tebbitt was faring.

The Yeovil Literary Prize

2013 Commended

Roger Elkin *Eddie's Mozart Bequest*	155
Sarah Hilary *My Father's Daughter*	157
Alan Ward *Negative*	162
Bruce Harris *Emily's Derby*	163
Louise Walford *At Prospero's Funeral*	168
Sandy Hogarth-Scott *The Boy*	169
Rowena Warwick *Body*	174
Fiona Mitchell *UFO Dad*	175
Michael Casey *The Shape of Rain*	180
Dru Marland *Zephyr*	181
Siobhan Collins *Stain Removal*	182
Marcus Smith *I Am Human and I Want To Confess*	186

EDDIE'S MOZART BEQUEST *by Roger Elkin*

For My friend, if and when he'd penned in ink
on the pink post-it sellotaped inside
the frontispiece. Surely he didn't think

by that *if* he'd survive while others died?
After all, he'd been near to death before:
as a child coughing up gobbings of blood

like flowers; and later, soldiering, he saw
several squaddies serving alongside him
dis-limbed and killed in furnaces of war:

Lucky escape, he'd quipped. *Wasn't my time
just then – still to come*, though knew not *never*
despite hiding behind that *if* – a form

of lying. It was the *when* he'd mither
about all day, then long into the night
once he'd stopped work, werriting on whether

he'd be hospitalized, or perhaps might
*drop off the perch while driving, hurt other
folk,* or fade away, alone, out of sight.

So, to save his wife unneeded bother
at his death, he'd signed this facsimile
cataloguing Mozart's output over

to me. Inside the book's wallpapery
sleeve, page following page of neat ruled staves
record the music's tread in spidery

notes. Good to see that though Mozart contrives
to tie invention down by penning list
in tempi, bars, key signatures, octaves

there's no *if and when* for him. Optimist,
he'd planned his notebook to reach far in time
for, balancing what he's scored, there's almost

as many empty pages: *Death defined
by absences.* I'm thrilled to get this book -
Eddie's bequest – better by far than mine:

these words. But suspect Eddie might not like
such notes; want silences to chart his wake.

MY FATHER'S DAUGHTER *by Sarah Hilary*

My father's driver does not have a name, not one I am allowed to use. If I need his attention, I must press the intercom in the back of the car. I must only press it in an emergency. If I need him to pull over, for instance, because I feel unwell and might be sick. I must not press the intercom just because I want to talk about my day, or because it is lonely in the back of the car.

My father's driver wears a peaked cap with a polished brim. The back of his neck is wide and strong. He is not yet old, perhaps thirty years. He wears his uniform well. My leotard does not suit me. Pink and black do not go together, whatever my father says. The hairband's lumpy across my cornrows. When I peel my bare shoulders away from the buttoned seat, my skin makes a kissing sound.

'Good morning, miss,' my father's driver says.

'Good morning,' I answer.

His hair is newly cut today and I see that he was hiding a tattoo at the back of his neck, a bird with its wings spread. I do not know the name of the bird, but I think perhaps it is a hawk. The tattoo is ink-blue. It wouldn't show against my skin.

I am pink in places, but nowhere my father's driver can see. Sometimes I pretend to practice an arabesque, so I can show the palms of my hands, which are almost pink. He meets my eyes in the mirror and smiles, before looking away.

Soldiers guard the doors to the embassy, rifles worn like sashes across their bodies. My father's driver is smoking with the soldiers. I watch him from my window. He has taken off his peaked cap and his uniform jacket, rolled up the sleeves of his shirt. There is another bird on his forearm, where the muscle winds like a rope. I cannot see from this distance, but I think it is an eagle. One of the soldiers has the same tattoo on his arm.

So now I think my father's driver must be a soldier. Maybe he has a gun and is under orders to shoot anyone who tries to take me from the street outside the ballet class.

I would like to be taken from the street, for the rebels to try and take me, the ambassador's black daughter – and for my father's driver to rescue me, put me under his arm while he fires his gun into the crowd. Of course I would not really like it. Not the gun. Just the arm. I would like his arm.

I breathe into the window and make a heart with my little finger.

All the glass in the embassy windows is shatterproof, after the last attack. The rebels are getting desperate, my father says. Desperate for what? I ask, but he says it was not intended for my ears. 'Simone,' he says and plants his hand on my head, his fingers thin between my corn rows. It is not my name. It is the name he has for me.

He is getting old. He may be called home any day now. I think he will take me with him, but I am not sure. He is only my father on paper. He says it is the same, but I know it is not. 'Who will drive me in London?' I ask.

He smiles. 'In London, you will take the bus.'

***

The ambassador's daughter, Simone, that's not her real name.

Her father's driver, Belloc, he knows.

The kid's real name is Nasiche. It means *born in the locust season*. Belloc knows this because her father asked him to witness the paperwork for the adoption, the day he went to the village. Belloc doesn't think the ambassador meant to come home with a child, but he didn't speak on the way down there, so maybe he was planning it all along. Little black scrap of a thing in a yellow blanket. The ambassador's not married. Belloc doubts they'd have let him adopt a child anywhere but here.

Ten years ago, give or take. She'll be twelve soon, nearly grown up. Belloc doesn't think she knows her real name, or that her brothers and sisters were taken from their home the same day she was, only not by the ambassador. Her brothers and sisters were taken by the rebels calling themselves the Lord's Army.

All the children in her village were stolen, one way or another.

When Belloc drives her to class, she sets her big eyes on the street, on the dust that coats the car, and the people she's been taught to fear. The car windows are tinted so she can see out but no one can see in. Sometimes they pass kids stirring sticks at the dust, making pictures. Belloc hears the ambassador's daughter drumming on the carpeted floor in the back of the car with the rosy soles of her feet.

She is like a slim stick of pink dynamite in here.

Each morning, her father pins an orchid to her leotard. 'For luck in class.'

In the car, she unpins it and peels its petals with her fingers before treading the orchid into the carpet. Belloc makes a point of not seeing her do this. The car smells like decay the same colour of her ballet uniform, sickly.

On the way home from class, she points at a squatting boy and says he is starving. 'No wonder they are getting desperate.'

Their eyes meet in the mirror.

Belloc is under orders not to talk to her about the rebels, the danger which is packed around the Embassy like explosives.

They sneak in the back way. Belloc lets her punch the code at the gate. He shouldn't, but he does. It is the only thing that makes her smile.

She works hard at the ballet, although she hates it. She would work hard at whatever she was put to. If Belloc was a poet instead of a soldier, he would say that the ambassador's daughter is made of orchids and industry.

'There is nothing to eat,' the ambassador's daughter decides, after searching the big fridge in the kitchen. 'Only eggs and milk.' She wrinkles her nose.

Belloc takes off his jacket. 'I can make doughnuts.'

She sits on the table, swinging her feet, as he beats the egg and whisks milk with a fork. He can't find a cutter for the dough, so he uses a cup. The doughnuts come up golden, puffed with sugar dust.

She doesn't speak until they are eating. 'These are good.' She holds up the doughnut, looking at him through the hole he made. 'I see you,' she says.

Her father is afraid she'll find out he stole her. He's never spoken about it, not to Belloc, but Belloc thinks he knows the way it was: the man wanted one small victory, to mark his time here. Or perhaps he only wanted one less recruit for his enemy.

That night, they discuss security, her father and those tasked with his safety. 'Trips out of the embassy should be limited to essential visits only.'

'Yes,' her father says, 'but it is different for Simone. She must go to her ballet classes. It is where her friends are.'

There is no arguing with him. It's as if he's dismissed them already.

Belloc has nowhere to go when his boss returns to London, no prospect of a job. No home or family. He'd be better off staying put, chancing his arm with the military. Except the thought of it makes him queasy, makes him remember how he once pissed his pants in fright because a thing flew from a tree into his face. Bats, warm and squirming, like the sky splitting into bits.

The next morning, against all their advice, Belloc takes Simone to her class.

They arrive late because the streets are filling with people, mostly children. This is the way of it, with the rebels. They send children ahead. The hairs on the back of Belloc's neck stand up and the blood pricks in his fingers.

He remembers heat pressed like a blank face to every window, boiling metal and bullets, the red stench of death, burrowing everywhere. Men with their guts held like infants in their arms.

'If we had any courage,' he thinks, 'we'd take the children off the streets. But we're afraid. So we pretend that they're just kids, even though we know most of them have guns and grenades and would use them without a second thought.'

'Take me home,' Simone says, when her ballet class is over.

She's shivering in the leotard, despite the heat; the car's caught in traffic and the air conditioning's sharp, like breathing metal. Belloc turns it off and opens a window. To do this, he has to cut the electrics that control the central locking, just for a second, but it's enough for her to shove open the door and dart out.

'Simone!' He's out of the car, chasing her on foot through the streets.

In that ballet uniform she should be easy to spot, but the crowd of kids has swallowed her whole.

He runs until the dust is packed into his lungs and then he stops, propping his fists on his knees, hunching over in a narrow alley strung with washing and outlawed flags striped in red, black and blue.

Belloc punches the code into the gate at the back of the Embassy, cursing because she knows the code. He gave it to her, despite his training.

Secure the perimeter, he thinks, *you arsehole.*

'You had one job to do,' her father, the ambassador tells him, '*one job.*'

The man looks haggard. This stops Belloc from saying that they warned him, about trips outside. He, not Belloc, should've kept her safe. That's his job, her father's. He will always have that job.

Belloc has nothing, after this. He'll be lucky to get a bouncer's gig, back in London. It ends for him here.

He leaves her father making phone-calls and goes outside for a smoke with the soldiers. They humour him, make sympathetic noises about the girl, but Belloc knows what they're thinking: that he couldn't even keep a kid safe in this shithole. He stays until the light bleeds out over the roofs opposite. Then he walks around the side of the Embassy, to the kitchen. He needs a cold drink.

The back door's off its hinges, hanging like a broken tooth.

Belloc can hear shouting inside, but it's at the front of the building. Back here, it's quiet. He's holding his breath, because he knows what's inside.

She's come back, and she's not alone.

He doesn't run. He doesn't shout.

Shouldering the door aside, he steps into the kitchen.

Some of the kids are in camouflage, cut-down to fit their skinny frames. The rebels' flag is stitched to their chests, red and black and blue. At least a dozen of them stand crowded around her.

She's handing out food from the fridge. Her fingers are stained and wet. She's still in her ballet uniform, pink leotard and cross-over cardigan, chiffon skirt and satin shoes.

She meets Belloc's eyes. He doesn't look away.

Her thin chest rises and falls. She lifts her hand and licks sugar from her thumb. She's feeding them doughnuts.

One of the kids pulls something from his pocket, a grenade or a gun.

Belloc doesn't take his eyes off the ambassador's daughter.

A hot, sour dust blows in through the broken door, opening the petals of her skirt, freckling the satin toes of her shoes with soot.

He says her name. 'Nasiche,' and puts his hands in the air, empty and open.

Her big eyes hold his across the room.

Above the tap of the gun's chamber, he says, very softly, 'I see you.'

NEGATIVE *by Alan Ward*

The stars look down on a spatter of smart phones,
a palm-chained system
tracing paths and alleyways
with white string – joining yellow streetlights
dot-to-dot. Of an evening, headlights
and stairwells strike out,
puff the air with white fog.
Buses whinny and whistle, ferry chunks of day.
We light trees and castles,
and, almost unintentionally,
paving slab cracks and streetlamp necks.
Between them, we are negative.
A woman with a pram slipping into nothing
between yellow pools, swelling into existence
with the next gush of light.
A dog, fox, exists for a few beats
and then is taken, nullified by the dark.
The light has power:
cars pass and pull houses and rooms into being,
never more than a wall or two at a time.

EMILY'S DERBY *by Bruce Harris*

Epsom Cottage Hospital, Sunday June 8th 1913

Behind the high rectangles of the ward windows, one bed in particular seemed to be singled out for particular attention. Curtains had been carefully drawn around it; inquiries from other patients were politely but firmly resisted. Enough gossip had managed to circulate to confirm the slight build and intense injuries of the patient, and other ladies who had seen the battered body being brought in four days previously were still exchanging shocked speculations as to what could possibly have happened to have brought about such damage to a young woman.

For the first two days, the myriad of disgraceful possibilities were thoroughly investigated in whispered, hesitant conversations, and the determined silence of the hospital staff provided a rich void for scurrilous tales of degeneracy and violence linked to vice. Some ladies began to feel the inquiries should be made concerning the likelihood of infections being introduced into the hospital from a woman of low birth, or conceivably even worse, low moral standing.

'This is no place whatever for a woman of the streets, however damaged, though the damage is no doubt consequent on a life in the criminal underworld,' Mrs. Mannington said, her back erect against the unforgiving brass of her bedhead and her nightdress drawn fully up to her neck as ever.

Sister Kate Allerton heard this remark as she passed through her ward, and wished, not for the first time, that her hearing was not as acute as it constantly seemed to be.

She quelled Mrs. Mannington with a look. The woman had arrived in the hospital with a badly sprained back, supposedly from humping heavy loads around the grocer's shop she kept with her husband. Kate was one of the few people who knew the real story of her back, let loose by a garrulous and less circumspect husband as a consequence of energetic love-making, 'and she not being as girlie supple as she used to be, you see,' A word or two into the patient community and Mrs. Mannington would find herself the butt end of much amusement. A different kind of woman would take it in her stride and even go as far as to brag about it, but Mrs. Mannington belonged to the breed of women who preferred to pretend that such things never happened, or if they did, were never to be spoken of in public. The 'lay down and think of England' brigade, as Kate thought of them.

Kate passed from the ward doors into the corridor, and Matron herself was standing almost directly in front of her; Matron was stout, dour and formidable, though Kate knew her well enough by now to know that much of that was a public front. She had needed her strength in recent days. The very next day after the young woman, whose name was Emily Davison, had been brought in, strange individuals, almost invariably men, had begun appearing on the spreading lawn in front of the hospital, and on two occasions so far, Matron had had to go out and insist that cameras be not set up on hospital premises. The following day, more men had appeared, and some women, and a few of them actually began to shout towards the hospital, occasionally employing language which Matron could scarcely believe could be uttered in a public place.

Matron directed Kate into a nearby store room, switched on the light and closed the door behind her.

'I even have to talk to people in rooms without windows, Kate. The situation is becoming impossible. We are fending off an endless stream of calls from the press; even when I insist that I will not have cameras near the hospital, they simply set them up on the other side of the road. Several men are actually watching us through binoculars. I have insisted on police protection, but there is a single semi-comatose constable in attendance, who is invariably not where he should be.'

Kate nodded sympathetically; she and Matron had established a firm bond, and while they did not entirely see eye to eye on the subject of female suffrage, they did entirely agree about professional ethics.

'I cannot take away several people from their normal duties, Kate, just to watch that Davison woman. Neither can I embark on any concentrated treatment; there is little we can do. In fact, Kate, between ourselves, there is nothing we can do but alleviate the pain as best we can. I need someone to guard the woman, and I want it to be you, Kate. I want you to stay with her at all times, and immediately call for help if there is any attempt on the part of any outside body to get near the woman. We have actually found,' Matron's eyes clouded and her hand almost shook beside her, Kate could never recall her being so moved, 'some men trying to gain illicit access to the hospital from the rear. I will see to it that all the other duties on your ward are attended to, Kate, and try and get our less than enthusiastic policeman to stand guard outside the ward. I would like you, please, to go to the Davison woman and stay with her at all times. I will be for ever in your debt. In the meantime, I must fend off the callers, which are beginning to include some of her fellow suffragettes, drum up more police presence if I can and continue to track down her own family.'

They left the store room and Matron went so far as to grab Kate's hand.

'Bless you, Kate. I suspect the crisis will not be long in duration, but while it lasts, we must all stick to our guns.'

Kate made her way straight to the heavy curtains surrounding Emily Davison's bed. She looked down at the slightly built body, almost girlish in its slenderness, though the records showed that the patient was actually forty years old. Miss Davison's features were very pale under the heavy bandages around her fractured skull. Her whole body was ominously still; Kate felt the pulse and it was very weak indeed. Kate's nursing instinct was to shout for help immediately, but she suppressed it; Matron was right, as she tended to be. The woman's injuries were such that there was nothing to be done. At least Emily's pale face did not look as if she was in pain, more in the throes of a long, deep sleep.

Kate, while not a suffragette herself in the teeth of the intractable opposition to the whole idea of women voting from her parents and her brother, knew something of Emily Davison from an old school friend who **was** a suffragette. If Emily was in pain, she would be used to it by now. In 1909, serving a month's hard labour for throwing rocks at the carriage of Chancellor David Lloyd George, Emily had so outraged a warder by barricading her cell that he had thrust a hose through the window and tried to drown her. In the nick of time, the door was broken down; Emily, typically, sued the prison and won no less than forty shillings.

In June 1912, serving a six month sentence in Holloway prison for alleged arson, Emily, like many of the other suffragettes, went on hunger strike against their treatment. The result was that they were regularly force fed, meaning a whole group of men held her down, forced a pipe through her teeth and into her throat and then sent food and drink down it. Emily stopped it, for herself and the others, by throwing herself down a ten metre iron staircase, causing herself head and spinal damage, clear enough when her clothes were removed.

Emily was once a teacher, it seemed. Now, to great outrage, including those foul-mouthed idiots on the hospital lawn, everyone seemed to have decided that Emily was attempting to attack the King's horse Anmer when she dashed out during the annual Epsom Derby at Tattenham Corner four days earlier. In her clothing, she had concealed a banner for the Women's Social and Political Union. Nobody really knew, Kate thought, exactly what her intentions were, but in the clatter of Derby horses, Kate could not really believe it would have been possible for her to identify the King's horse. She meant to put the banner somewhere, or attach it to something, but it did not logically follow that it would be to a horse. However, Emily's reputation was such that many people would attribute the worst motives to her if they could, which perhaps said more about them than it did about Emily.

There was something resembling a sigh, an exhausted exhalation of most of the breath Emily had left, and Kate knew the moment was now imminent. The noisy wood and metallic clatter of a sizeable carriage at the front of the hospital suggested that friends or visitors were arriving, and Kate felt a pang of pity at their untimely lateness. She moved one of Emily's hands into hers, and a resolution formed implacably in her mind.

She was going to join the WSPU. She might not be able to chain herself to railings or endure force feedings, but she could help in the quiet ways where she could be most effective – organisation, distributing literature, perhaps even treating injuries after demonstrations. She could no longer stand aside, as the Mrs. Manningtons of the world did, and pretend this problem wasn't her problem.

Leaving home would be inevitable. Her headmaster father was an expert on suppressing conversational subjects of which he disapproved, and in any case, he thought or spoke of little else but the war he was convinced was approaching. Her mother equally forbade 'disputatious' subjects from the home, 'and especially at meal tables.' Her brother Ralph would have brief sparring sessions with her on the subject when neither parent was present, which saddened her, because they got on well in almost every other respect, and Ralph was far from stupid; she could not understand why he wouldn't see the simple justice of votes for women.

'Tell me, Kate,' he hissed at her one morning, when Father had left his newspaper open at a page once again speculating about the theoretical coming war, 'if women do get the right to vote, will they vote to go and fight the war, as the men will have to?'

'Ralph,' she said, smiling faintly as she buttered her toast, 'if the women of Britain and Germany had the vote, there wouldn't be a war to fight.' For once, her brother found himself countered enough to at least pause for thought.

Emily's hand was very cold. Kate felt that she should say something, mark this moment in some acknowledging or affirming way. 'Shame!' some outraged and very loud male voice shouted from the hospital lawn. Shame indeed, Kate thought, a crying shame for the waste of it.

What will they eventually call it, I wonder, she thought. So many of them will curse and splutter at the fact of it, the supposed attack on the King's horse, the sudden madness of a deluded woman. Perhaps no-one will remember the horse or the owner who won it, or the weather, or which distinguished personages were amongst the crowd. Perhaps they will turn Emily into some sinister agent intent on damaging royal interests. But, for me, it will always be Emily's Derby, and it will be

Emily's cause which I will remember most, a cause which I now pledge myself to support. Emily's last day in her cause will be almost the same as my first.

The ward door had opened and both light and heavy footsteps were approaching. Emily's hand went colder still; the pulse was very weak now. Kate kissed the stony cheek and stood up to welcome the visitors.

AT PROSPERO'S FUNERAL *by Louise Walford*

My father wept when he left his dainty Ariel
behind. Half-blind with grief, he stood in the stern
of Alonso's ship, watching the isle dissolve.
Ariel's farewell breath filled the sails; he flickered
in cold flames along the spars and rigging, danced
like an ape atop the crow's nest. But all my father
did was weep and stare.
    It's there I see him now,
hands whitely gripping a salt-roughened rope,
his robe becoming watercolours as the island fades.
His old eyes crust with cataracts, spine bends,
nose hooks, cheeks shrink. He looks his age.
No more the mage who raised the dead, controlled
the stir and sweep of the wind, brought goddesses
to earth.
    But then, it always *was* a show - always
the cliff-top pose, cloak billowing behind, staff
raised. The ducal voice. *I am Milan.* He was a fake,
my bully father. It was Ariel who could change
for the occasion, slip into a mermaid's skin,
vanish to a drift of pipe and tabor in the air.

I'd tear the stinking feathers from his harpy's wings.
I'd trap him tight in the oak's entrails. He'd not
entangle me in his foul song, the changeling thief.

My father thought I didn't know. The mighty Prospero
relying on a wisp of spirit! Mastering him with a promise.
He never promised me. He turned me off and on.
Fed me to Ferdinand, the sap, to stitch together Naples
and Milan. I was a child. How did I know the world
had such men in it?
    No, it was his dainty chick, his Ariel,
for whom he wept and stared. I was just his blood.
No good ever came from daughters. So I watched him,
clung to his words as if they'd raft me home, studied
his ageing face as it corrugated and dissolved.
But it was Ariel he wept for.

THE BOY *by Sandy Hogarth-Scott*

1.
The boy sits at his end of the table, near the large window overlooking the sea. It is his territory: for his books or schoolwork or just for sprawling in the hard wooden chair, elbows on the table watching her cook.

He wears the same clothes as he wore yesterday and several days before. Washing barely creates a distinguishing ripple. His clothes shrink a little and he grows a little. He doesn't feel the hard wood of the chair beneath his muscled bum but his left elbow itches where he has leant on it too long. He moves his arm, scratches the dry skin and watches. The dog lies on the hard stone floor, his black nose and light brown head millimetres from the boy's feet. He too watches.

She grows warm from the wood stove and from the boy's liquid brown eyes. She's his mother but he calls her Martha, occasionally 'mum' and then he notices an incipient smile around the edges of her lips and faint wrinkles in the corners of her eyes.

In bad times the boy thinks she's a witch. He doesn't know other women and girls are a mystery. His mother tells him that he'll leave her soon enough.

She thinks of him as 'the boy' but named him Ned. She likes short names, the paring down to essentials.

2.
They live in a house by the sea, a solitary house 150 miles from anywhere. City dwellers would think it savage, lacking grace and refinement, but it is solid, purposeful, built of dressed stone and topped with a tin roof. It was made to last, to hold families of hard-working men and child bearing women and all that went with that and more: the house cow to milk, the chickens to feed and protect and the scrawny heat blasted vegetable patch to weep over.

The interior is divided, with workmanlike precision, into four equal squares. The kitchen and sitting room face the sea. Two bedrooms are at the back: hers furnished with a double bed for her lonely sleep, his with two narrow beds. He sleeps in one and piles his clothes on the other.

The rooms have large windows and stay cool in the long hot summers. A broad veranda runs around all four sides of the house, providing, in its deep recesses and shadows, shelter from the destroyer sun. In times of wind the boy and his mother huddle in the kitchen.

At the back the veranda is walled off with wood and fitted with a small bath that the boy soon outgrows, although she does not, and a washbasin and a lavatory. The waste runs underground to a pit 50 yards away. It has never been emptied.

The only out building is a shed which houses half a dozen scraggy fowls and a rooster too hot or too bored to strut or crow. Heavy stones hold down the tin roof. Outside, dirt stretches, flat and languorous, into the distance.

3.

Searing heat mutates into slightly less hot. Rain shocks, a few downpours a year. There's a bore hole but she has no idea how long it will last so she is careful.

Just after sunrise the boy wakes, stretches, picks up towel and clothes and walks naked down the dirt path, past the battered car he longs to drive, and across the sand that doesn't yet burn his bare feet. The dog follows.

Today there's no onshore breeze, just smouldering stillness. Further out than the eye can clearly discern the blue/green sea segues into the horizon. He loves the sea. The fishermen speak of sharks but he's not afraid.

He swims, a smooth loping crawl, out and back again, troubling the water little, throwing his long hair from side to side, his arms moving strongly, smoothly, his feet fluttering.

He runs from the water, his body a patchwork of cream and deep brown. The night chill is still in the air so he throws on the tee shirt and mildly grubby shorts. Tomorrow is wash day.

Lately his thoughts are the same: what lies beyond the horizon, beyond the house. He asks his mother where he comes from. He can remember no other place.

'Here,' she says, and looks away.

4.

Further along the beach his mother watches. The boy knows she's watching.

She too has been up since dawn but it's not a good day for painting, won't be: empty harsh light. Morning shadows and uncertainty is what she yearns for.

Later, when the sun drives her in, she'll paint in the cool of the veranda, tinkering with the reality she's lost or found.

Sometimes, a cigarette hanging from her lips, she stares for minutes at a time at one colour squeezed onto her palette, a fat luminous slug. The boy asks her what she's looking at. She shakes her head, cannot say.

Then she'll paint quickly, a beginning.

She imagines them both when they're very old, doing the same things: he will swim, she will paint. But she only hopes.

They live their lives by the light, hesitant twilight or nervous faltering dawn and blinding bright days, not by the calendar, although one hangs on the wall, the only tangible reminder of passing time in a world not theirs.

He's home schooled. He discovers King Arthur and the Round Table and fashions Excalibur from a piece of driftwood. He wants to be a soldier, a traveller of the world beyond his sea. She is a classicist so she nurtures him on the Iliad and the Odyssey and he calls himself Odysseus. For a time.

Sometimes a boat anchors off their beach and she buys fish. The fishermen stay a while, offer to take the boy, teach him to fish. He doesn't know if he wants to go but she encourages him.

After one trip he asks her about his father. 'Gone,' she says and looks away. He can tell by the expression on her face that she will not say more.

5.

When he was very young his mother told him that a baby grows in its mother's tummy. She spoke of a young woman whose baby grew from her sister's egg, not from her own. The boy thought of chickens and didn't understand. The sister, his mother said, claimed that the child was hers, from her egg and took the child to bring up herself. The young woman waited then stole the child back.

'Was she a witch?' he asked but was not really interested.

She's his mother. He grew inside her. She was not a young mother: 38. That made her sisterly gift immeasurably more generous. Both women worried about what it meant to be a mother.

Her twin sister Rosamund claimed him, said that the child grew from her egg and the sperm of the man she selected, that her sister had merely loaned her womb.

Rosamund is rich. She buys and sells houses and lives on the other side of the world. She had her son's life planned out.

For a week or two the sisters shared the mother role. Martha thought she might live nearby, keep watch but when she could stand it no longer she left to go far away. Then the day after the boy's second birthday she returned, secretly, to her sister's mansion and carried him off to a place her sister would never find, to the house by the sea.

6.

Martha drives into town when the boy goes fishing: for food and for the boy's correspondence course. There are no letters to collect. And for cigarettes. Lately the boy has started pinching her fags. She surmises only a couple a day and pretends she doesn't notice.

And she goes to town for sex, the sort of sex that doesn't go hand in hand with love. The man, her lover, is always pleased to see her.

It's the boy's 16th birthday. She gives him a painting of himself swimming out to sea. His long hair floats on the surface; he's a long way out. She has given him a painting on this day for the past 14 years. He hangs them in neat busy rows in his bedroom. They are snapshots of his life but he no longer really notices them. He's grown impatient, bored, and talks less although neither of them is much in the way of casual chatter. Once she filled his days with stories but that's past.

She is wearing a dress. He notices and is surprised. She tells him that she will take him to town and teach him to drive. He says 'Thanks, mum' and gives her a hug. She's happy.

He goes to his room to put on clean shorts and tee shirt and find some shoes.

The town has a short main street with a petrol station, a couple of pubs and a grocer who also sells newspapers, only two titles; a hardware store, a café with a one room bookstore at the back, a few other shops and a small plain wooden building that doubles as church and hall. Less than a couple of hundred houses cluster behind the street.

In town his eyes widen, his lips part. 'So many,' he says, looking down the wide street where fifteen or twenty cars are parked haphazardly. 'So many,' he repeats.

'What?' she says.

He motions to the cars, to the buildings. It is too hot for people to be out.

When she pulls up outside the cafe he doesn't get out but sits and gazes, his head swivelling.

'Come on,' she says, and opens his door, pulling gently on his arm. She leads him in, to the tables and chairs, old, crumbling. In the dark interior are shelves stacked with books. She's in a hurry. She turns her head and waves to the man behind the counter. 'Jack,' she tells the boy. 'He'll look after you until I come back. Are you hungry?' He nods, stuck for words. 'Have a feast. It's your birthday.' She motions towards the counter laden with huge filled rolls and large slabs of cake. 'I'll pay later.' Then she says, and he hears the urgency in her voice, 'Wait for me here.' She waves her hand towards the shelves of books. 'Choose some books. I'll be back.'

She pauses in front of the man called Jack. 'My son,' she says, pointing back to the boy. Then she hurries out and up the street. She doesn't see the astonishment on Jack's face or hear him start to say 'A woman...'

Her lover is waiting.

Much later she returns to the café and looks for the boy. There are only a couple of men sitting at one table. She half runs to the bookshelves. He's not there. She turns. Jack moves toward her, his big hands thrusting aside the fearful air and starts to speak. She pushes past him into the street. There's a note tucked under the car's windscreen wiper.

'The boy is mine.'

R.

She would recognise her sister's handwriting anywhere, although she hasn't seen it for a very long time.

BODY *by Rowena Warwick*

the drape misses the feet
like it's a hot night
the hallux, his big toe
the parcel tag hanging

my scalpel shines clean
unrolled from its canvas wrap
untainted by formalin
or lobules of solid fat

he lies here unashamed
his faults his triumphs
there is no dark corner
no robe or towel

around his nipples
fine grey hair thins
here the stump of his penis
flattened against hard scrotum

should I be seeing this?
is this how he expected it to be?
unblushing, him,
not me, while my gloves

touch this skin
lived in, caressed
soaped and powdered
kissed and slapped

UFO DAD *by Fiona Mitchell*

My dad wants to be abducted by aliens so we've been doing these midnight picnics for years.

He is clambering over the turnstile now, putting his hand out to steady me as I stamp down the planks whorled with age.

The air is wet, grassy, perfumed with bracken. A hidden stream sprays through a mossy crevice. The hill hurts my calves and I lag behind Dad whose head tilts towards the waning moon, silvering his frenzied hair.

Music spills from Dad, a one-time guitarist in a band. It thumps in his leg-tapping fingers. It hums from his newly bladed neck. He whistles a tune I don't recognise.

I run to catch him up, my feet churning the soil. He turns and smiles. I unzip the bag, parachuting the checkered blanket. Dad tidies the edges and we sit.

It will be a while before the damp saturates the tartan. I've wrapped myself up for the cold: two thermal vests, long johns, sheepskin mittens, a hot water bottle clamped into my waistband.

'Like a lagged pipe,' Joan had said as she saw us off at the cottage door.

Dad pulls out binoculars, a notebook. I remove the Thermos from the bag, set the torn packet of crisps between us.

These Saturday night excursions started when I was a kid. Fruit cake in foil, frozen fingers, a stomach full of soup.

It was finding the crop circle that kept us going. Wading through wheat, stumbling upon the flattened expanse. We stepped into it, staring in disbelief at the perfect circle. I prized off my boots and traced it with my toes. Combing the straw, then smelling my fingertips for clues. We were dots in the centre, scissoring our legs like angels without snow.

The exhilaration radiated for months.

There were long summer evenings back then when Dad would come home from the ice cream factory and open a cardboard box packed with dry ice on the lawn. The vapour curled and wafted signals through the air as we unloaded King Cones, Mivvis, Lolly Gobble Choc Bombs.

Mother walked out on us when I was four. She upped sticks for America, found herself a trader, made a new family with my half brother Erik and his little sister. When Erik said he hated the way his late mother used to hug him so hard, it was a stranger he was talking about. She was cardboard stiff in the picture beside my bed, the one I'd tuck into a drawer only to find it later propped back where it was.

I went out to see Mother once, but it was like lifting a scab to find it hadn't healed beneath. She went back to being that cigarette-toting woman in yellowed photographs. There's still a shoe box full of them in the loft.

And so our life went on. Dad waiting out of sight around a corner when I went to parties, ferrying each of my friends home in his car.

He can't sit still, my dad. At parents' evening once, as his knees jigged under the desk, my maths teacher said I had a bad case of endoftermitis. Dad looked that up in Encyclopaedia Britannica when he got home.

Tonight, cars whir on the distant motorway, our soundtrack in the dark. We sit on the highest of the hills, peer at the navy sky. The wind picks up, lifting leaves.

I pour me and Dad metallic tea.

'That's Pegasus over there,' he points at the sky. I conjure up faces and demons in the daisy chain of stars. 'See the Summer Triangle,' he says.

I nod, like I always do, but can't see those shapes. I don't believe in aliens either, but I've never told Dad that.

His second wife Joan joins us in the fields sometimes. When she does, we share a secret smile. 'Just you and your dad,' she said tonight as we walked from the door.

Joan had made a cake that didn't rise properly. 'Happy birthday, Frankie,' she said, leaving the pucker of her Fuchsia Blush on his cheek. 'Not a cake really. More of a biscuit,' she added as we ate the filings.

Earlier, Dad had strummed his electric guitar while Joan jigged around the living room in her pop socks. I crossed my legs, shook my head when Joan urged me up.

Dad peers at the star-peppered night without blinking, urging the heavens to show us something more, something to eclipse that time we sat amid the circle of hay.

'The triangular crafts of Rendlesham. That'd be nice,' he says then.

'What about Roswell?' I ask, knowing what's coming next.

'Absolute hogwash,' he rants through a mouthful of crisps. Dad has strong views on alien life forms.

'What do you reckon they look like?' I ask.

'Nothing you could imagine. Think bug eyes, reptilian skin, you'll probably be wrong. They might be shadow beings, like air...' he says, voice like toffee.

Thinking about extraterrestrials was scary when I was nine years old. I'd make Frank perch on the staircase while I went upstairs to the loo, mid-Doctor Who. We watched Space 1999, The Tomorrow People, Sapphire and Steel.

Dad photographed dark patches and dubious lights with his Colourflash De Luxe. But his 'raison d'être' as he calls it - he likes to flavour his conversation with French words - is to be taken and grilled by Martians.

'There are beings out there, light-years ahead in technology and intelligence,' he says.

I dab at the crumbs wedged into the corner of the crisp packet. The salt brings tears to my eyes.

'Do you miss playing for the crowd?' I ask.

'All those eyes staring up at me. Best bit was writing the songs - all that thinking. And afterwards, beer in hand. Deaf for days I was.

'Where would I rather be, eh - on stage, or here, space all around, with my Sandra, my creme de la creme?'

Dad would never have joined the Turbines if Johnny hadn't asked. Dad had invited Johnny and his wife for dinner. Two bottles of Black Tower, a burnt tea towel on the worktop from the flaming chip pan, later and Dad had plugged in his electric guitar with a jagged twang.

He leapt on to one knee and strummed as I stared through a crack in the door. The couple blocked their ears. Dad lowered the volume and gave a patchy rendition of Delbert McClinton's *Giving it Up for Your Love*.

'Flicking 'eck,' said Johnny, 'you're just what we're looking for...'

The Turbines played once a month at the Rising Sun in Silkstone, even had a gig in Huddersfield once. They recorded an album that sold 150 copies at Woolworths. 'Eagles,' it said in neon letters, and in the small print, 'sung by The Turbines.'

'It's a cover version,' Dad said then. 'Small steps, Sandra. Small steps.'

I thought he was writing poetry when I found him scribbling at the kitchen table, but he has exercise books full of songs. The Turbines recorded three of them, including *Look Back in Wonder* which used to fill the sprung dance floor at the Rising Sun.

Dad taught me to read music. At university, I'd take out my Yamaha Acoustic, close my eyes and strum.

I could hold a note, but I was never a dancer. Not like Dad. None of your dad dancing either. Frank can move. Whatever he does, air guitar or robotics, he looks good, even now he's seventy.

Back then, I stepped on to Dad's slippers and he danced me round the house. He caught my bare feet and tickled them as he chased me up the stairs. He sang me songs when I got bullied.

Then, Joan's soft rolls shot down the conveyer belt in Bejam, colliding with Dad's frozen beef burgers.

Joan had blushed. Dad had chortled. And a couple of weeks later, Joan sat on our sofa dueting with Dad. He sang while she did the echoey bits.

Dad snatches my polystyrene cup, slings the caffeine contents across the turf.

He pulls open his jacket, a shiny bottle of Asti Spumante pushed into an inside pocket.

'This is for us,' he says.

His fingers turn white with the pressure and the cork leaps into the air.

We clink cups and the bubbles go up my nose.

'I've got the best birthday present ever,' Dad says.

He's about to tell me how proud he is that I'm a vet. His eyes teared over when I got the job 20 miles from here.

'Took me a while, but I did it,' he says then. He's not talking about me.

'That pop group,' he says, making circles with his dripping cup, his hands collaged with age spots.

I take another sip of the sparkle.

'Trio of Men,' he says. 'They want to cover one of the songs that I wrote, *Look Back in Wonder*.' His milky eyes are a surprise.

The Asti Spumante jets from my mouth. I pat the droplets on my chin.

'The boy band?'

'That's the one,' says Frank.

I pick up the bottle, fill the cups to the top.

'Might finally be on Top of the Pops,' says Dad.

I pull off my mittens, sandpaper hands on my face.

When the band had their photograph taken for the Gazette, Dad had paced the floors for days, clenching his fists. The photograph had appeared on the front, Dad's eyes retreating into their sockets, his mouth twisted.

A distant helicopter throws a triangle of light. An owl hoots on a loop and faraway, things with wings flutter. I take an earthy breath. Plucking a dandelion, stalk and all, I squeeze it, pinpricks of juice on my fingertips.

I throw it to the side and push my hand into the bag. I press a button on the tape recorder I found in my old room.

The chords strike and Dad loses some of his drink over the cup's sides.

'You knew,' he says.

'About the deal? No,' I say, shaking my head.

I packed the tape recorder as an afterthought. When I realised how heavy the bag was, I almost took it out.

'When the stars align and all that...' I say.

His eyes are full of the wind. I stand up, let his hand cover mine.

His throaty young vocals fill the air. He shimmies his hips. I dance, air-denying laughter taking me. Then I stagger sideways and Dad jives me round.

I am doubled over, the nerves in my stomach taught. When I look up, he is spinning, anoraked arms splayed like wings, the moon strobing his smile. The light patterns his face and he is transformed, a stranger. He stops, then closes his eyes, his chest filling with air, his own private celebration.

His smile fades and he falls, an outsize starfish on the marshy grass.

'Dad!' I shout and run to him, my heel going sideways on a clod of earth. On my knees beside him, he smiles wide.

'Just wanted my name somewhere, that's all,' he says.

Another song begins and he gets up, moving his feet, twisting his body. In my head, Joan is saying, 'Sit down Frank, think of your stent.'

Dad curves his silhouette over the earth. His feet smack as if trying to dislodge something. He shuffles and stamps until a semi-circle is flattened in the grass.

He is standing on the edge of it, not like that halo of hay that we found all those years ago, but imperfect and squashed.

I run to him then, punching the air with my fist. I jump and Dad jumps higher still. We go forwards until we've completed a circle in the blades. Clouds swallow up the moon and Dad smiles in the shadows.

THE SHAPE OF RAIN *by Michael Casey*

Bruised purple clouds hang around, menacing
as night-club bouncers fondling knuckles;
the first drops are ominously large and heavy,
hitting the pavement like squashed sloes.
Smaller drops, riposting in coronets,
join forces as the tempo quickens,
make small magnetic jumps to coalesce
with other blinking eyes of mercury.

The glassy layer floods gutters already
filled by glutted drains; the khaki streams
begin to race; leaves sail by, and paper scraps
and ticket stubs all swept away in confluence,
a regatta of departing souls; the flail
of dancing feet whips up eruptions,
craters and ring-forts, until the hollows over-
flow; then ripples intersect and spread

out into wider gyres and fiddle-heads,
rush wildly down the slope, the pattern
lengthening into the grain of wood—
the cell memory of yew and ash.
Marionettes must continue the dance
on small sad feet until the strings break.

ZEPHYR *by Dru Marland*

I wonder how you always find your way back home.
I'm really small, in the back seat of the Zephyr that you drive,
And we're off to Preston, to the shops. But you went alone
That trip you never came back home from. You were thirty five.

We wandered in the wreckage of our grief for you
That hurts too much to think of, even yet.
When father met and married someone new
I felt betrayed he could so easily forget.

Which was of course unkind. With craftsman's touch,
He was forever building stuff and moving on,
And drank, as did we all, too often and too much.
And died. I wished we'd talked. That moment's gone.

I sometimes wonder what you'd think of how things went for me
And then recall the love. That's what matters. That is family.

STAIN REMOVAL *by Siobhan Collins*

In April Louisa had been a big deal on the West End. Her performance in the experimental play Knee did not impress the critics but she did gain some fanatical admirers. Her beauty was a factor, doubtless. The papers loved her. They called her a Nubian Queen. Originality is too great a hope, apparently, from the tabloids.

They wished her victory, because she was *theirs,* in her contentious celebrity divorce.

Audiences take an ownership from their involvement in the beauty, the gloss and glimmer, of the perfect face. It becomes more an aspect of life, like the weather or the political times, than the arrangement and relative scale of nose, eyeballs and lips.

Being owned by the public is no easy matter. It excludes any possibility of running down to the supermarket at nine-thirty on a Sunday morning in your velour pyjamas. Once the gossip columns get you, tired, blemished and only just awake, you might as well give up on your dreams and go back to finish your accountancy exams as your mother told you.

But the numbers had always fought her, repelling each other like so many electrically charged particles, so that balances were not balanced and figures differed when they should have come to accord. As an accountant, therefore, she would have been ridiculous. As an actress, she was less ridiculous and more adequate. As a beauty, and as a beauty alone, she was exceptional.

She would have wrinkled her elegant nose at this. She had ideas on artistry and wished the term applied to herself, simultaneously despising her own beauty and fearing its disappearance.

If she weren't beautiful, would she be nothing at all?

And now she was nothing at all. There is no beauty in death, other than in the symmetry of life ending, the body decomposing and other organisms finding in the dying matter the means by which to thrive.

That which was once Louisa lay, a collapsing structure of bone and muscle, in an empty bath.

They found her in the morning.

The first police officer on the scene was interested in theatre, so she recognised the astonishing face within a second or two. Its former loveliness was almost gone now. There was no life left to illuminate the dark eyes so they were merely dark. Her colleague, who had arrived just a few seconds after, whistled through his teeth. Celebrity murder was a curse for the police. The press would go mad. They would hover like insects. They would hamper and make a story of it.

Once, she had been a child, then an adult, then an actress (and there it begins) and now she was nothing more than an idea that could be fashioned into a multiplicity of ideas, depending on the writer.

After death, she could demand no input into this pinning down of the truths that constructed her.

The crime scene was cordoned off and scrutinised for several days. Then the cleaners came.

Alice Webb, who was such a cleaner, finished up on a Wednesday evening after a day in Louisa's apartment. She went back to her flat in Clapham and jabbed her key into the lock. She was tired and dirty and knew that this was one of *those* cases. It irritated her that she could not stop her work from coming home with her.

It was not that she hated her job, although it was hard work, lifting the stains. They were so obstinate, resistant, ruining sheets and paintwork and beautiful wooden floors. And, in a way, she was proud of the work because she knew that her service was valuable, providing, if not comfort, then at least no fresh injury for the bereaved. For them, she made her application of cleansing chemical all the more vigorous. She would have liked to rub it all away, all evidence of the event. *That* was impossible, of course. But she did try.

She thought sometimes that the liquid in the stains moved though the protective clothing and into her skin as she cleaned. Then it stayed with her, on the inside.

Anyway, it was not the work, the scrubbing away - the dissolving of the marks of violence, that disturbed the tranquilly of her nights. The others, she felt quite sure, could exclude these thoughts, of damage and sleaze and wounded, abused flesh, so that they did not colonise their private hours.

It would be nice if she were *allowed* to do this.

At quarter to eight, Alice woke. She congratulated herself on a full night of sleep. Usually it was more difficult.

In the kitchen, there was a woman. She was sitting at the breakfast bar, silently drumming her fingers against the colourful tiles. She had been waiting here for a while, she said, but had not liked to wake anyone up. People need their sleep, she added, while Alice filled the kettle and ground the coffee. Alice did not offer the woman coffee. Why did they just let themselves in like that? One day, one of them would knock at the door and actually *ask* to come in, she thought.

"Don't do that sarcasm," The woman spoke with Caribbean melody in her voice. "You know I can't knock..."

She demonstrated, rapping the table twice, so that her knuckles vanished into the surface, as if the tiles were made of liquid.

"You don't look like yourself," Alice interrupted. "You were at least five inches taller before. And your face was different."

The woman sighed, as if she were obliged to explain an abstract concept to a small child.

"Why would I take *that* on again?" She asked. "It was bad enough the first time. I'm bored sick of beauty. Beauty. It's not real beauty, you know. Only skin. And skin isn't all that important to me. Not now. If you'd prefer, I could be male. Would that be better? Makes no difference to me, girl. There's no *eternal feminine* here. Or *eternal masculine* either. Why does everyone think that?"

She considered this.

"I suppose it suits them... "

She flickered, and reappeared as a man. Caucasian, he was, with whitish stubble. He patted his ample stomach with satisfaction. Evidently the sensation of being well-fed was a new one. Beautiful female celebrities cannot really eat, after all. He smiled, revealing the gap between the front teeth. She had been celebrated, before, for that gap. Some things are more difficult to cast off, perhaps.

What philosophers they were, Alice was thinking. If they were really here, why did they not come out with whatever they wanted to say? It would be simpler, and faster. They always had something to say - who killed them, or whatever.

Louisa allowed his chunky white male form to spin on the bar stool.

"Yes, you're right there." She/He/It said. "It was my solicitor. Martin Bradlet, of *Bradlet and Talley*. I suppose you might call him a sociopath, although you'd never guess it. I didn't... He liked it, I think, so he'll probably do it again, to someone else. It's not about revenge though. You'd think that I'd hate him, wouldn't you... But I don't. I don't even know him. I'm so far away now, you see... And it's not as if he can do me any harm. But my father is feeling it. So is Mum. It might make things a bit better..."

"On the other hand, it probably won't."

Alice wished, again, that they would find some-one else to orchestrate their *post-mortem* campaigns. She could, it is true, decide that it was not her business. Not say a word. Maybe the police would work it out by themselves. But then she would have visitations every night.

They were generally polite, apart from the trespassing, but they became sullen and moody when they felt themselves ignored.

And anyway, the police were not always so very resourceful.

"Just don't be a fool, you." Louisa said. "Send them a note telling them that you saw him leaving the building. At half-past three in the morning. That would be right... You don't have to sign it... Do it soon... He hasn't burned my things yet. They're a bit of a mess..."

She paused, remembering. Then she shook her head, as if shaking the memory into small pieces.

Alice sighed. She could do nothing else.

"Thanks pet." The apparition was restored to full, sweet humour. She was also back in female form, although she was now of Maori appearance, and tall. She turned, as if she were about to leave.

"What did you think of it, by the way?" She asked. "I mean that play - *Knee*?"

The hunger for approval persists then, even in the afterlife.

"I thought it was terrible." Alice answered. "But you were fantastic in it."

It was only half a lie.

Louisa nodded and then she vanished, slowly.

You might as well say something nice, if you have to say something, Alice thought.

I AM HUMAN AND I WANT TO CONFESS *by*
Marcus Smith

Let moods be random chemicals, then. I'll wait
For hate to neurotransmit set laws,
Presume rage means enzymes and will abate
As soon as they dissolve and not because
Of any thought or choice that comes from me.
So too with joy and love, grief or anger –
All fermenting accidents as empty
As bubbles. Bubbling on, I surrender
My will and can shrug off the terrible crime
As the whim of unfortunate biology.
(Comfort also for my victims, experts stress.)
But, Ladies and Gentlemen, now it's my time:
I did those things and more. Condemn *just me*.
I am human and I want to confess.

BIOGRAPHIES

Chris Allen

Chris Allen is a Technical Author with a degree in Physics and many years of experience working as a contractor throughout the United Kingdom in such industries as Avionics, Defence and Transport. He is also a Hypnotherapist and is a full member of the British Society of Clinical Hypnosis. He is married and lives in Hampton, Middlesex. Web site: www.cach.co.uk

Graham Anderson

Graham Anderson was born in London and has worked mainly as a theatre translator. His publications include plays by Feydeau and Beaumarchais. As a fiction reviewer he has written for City Limits, The Independent and The Sunday Telegraph. His own short fiction has twice been short-listed for literary prizes. He lives in Oxfordshire.

Chrissy Banks

Chrissy Banks was born in the Isle of Man and now lives in Somerset. Her poems are in magazines such as the Rialto and the North, and various anthologies, most recently *The Captain's Table* and *The Listening Walk*. A collection, *Days of Fire & Flood*, is out of print. Her website is www.chrissybankspoetry.com

Mike Bannister

Mike Bannister was born in Worcestershire. Following military service, he worked in Community Schools, mostly in the inner-cities. He now lives in Suffolk, where he chairs *Café Poets at Pinky's* a venue for working poets. Publications: *Greenstreet Fragments* (2003), *Pocahontas in Ludgate* (2007), *Orinsay Poems* (2012). His work has appeared in magazines regionally and nationally, earning a variety of awards and commendations.

Sue Belfrage

Sue Belfrage works in publishing. In her free time, she enjoys writing and painting. She lives in south Somerset.

Sharon Black

Sharon Black is originally from Glasgow but now lives in the Cévennes mountains of southern France where she organizes creative writing retreats (www.abricreativewriting.com). Her poetry has been published widely. In 2013 she won Ilkley Literature Festival Poetry Competition and was runner-up in the Troubadour Poetry Prize. Her collection, To Know Bedrock, is published by Pindrop Press. www.sharonblack.co.uk

Eve Bonham

Eve Bonham is the author of 2 books: a collection of short stories "Madness Lies and Other Stories" (2008) and a novel about female friendship "To the End of the Day" (2011), published in hardback and in a Kindle edition. She is working on her next book "Theo." She lives in Dorset, writes fiction, paints watercolours and plants trees.

J A Brooks

Born in Hampshire, J A Brooks was married at nineteen, and widowed at thirty-eight with four children. She met like-minded people at a creative wring class, and they eventually formed The Café Club Writers that produces a small booklet theree times a year called 'Short Stories and Tall Tales'. The proceeds from this go to the charity Macmillan Nurses.

Beryl Brown

Beryl has been living and writing in Dorset for over a decade. She lives with her husband and a Dalmatian, and enjoys visiting her daughter in London. She has had short stories published, some competition successes and is currently studying for a BA with the Open University. A novel is in progress.

Michael Casey

Michael Casey was educated in New Ross, University College Dublin, and the University of Cambridge where he earned a Ph. D. He has taught and worked in Dublin, Cambridge, Washington D.C. and the Caribbean Basin. He has published three books and a considerable volume of poetry and short fiction, much of it award-winning. A couple of his plays have been performed. He has published hundreds of articles in the Irish Times, Sunday Times and other journals.

Catherine Chanter

Catherine Chanter was winner and runner up in the Yeovil Literary Prize in 2010 and her poetry and short stories have appeared in a wide range of publications. Her novella Rooms of the Mind was published by Cinnamon Press in 2011 and her first full length novel, The Well won the Lucy Cavendish Fiction Prize, 2013 and will be published by Canongate early in 2015 with foreign publishing deals confirmed in nine other countries.

Siobhan Collins

Siobhan Collins works in an office for a public body in Cork, Ireland. She likes to write stories that graft the bizarre onto the ordinary, making worlds where there is nothing odd about oddness. She writes during her free time. There's never enough of *that*, of course.

Hilary Davies

Hilary Davies is a poet, translator and critic. She is the author of three collections of poetry from Enitharmon. She won an Eric Gregory Award for Young Poets (1983), has been a Hawthornden Fellow, was 1st prizewinner in the Cheltenham Literary Festival Poetry competition (1987), and Chairman of the Poetry Society (1992-3). Hilary taught French and German in secondary school for 28 years, and is now RLF Fellow in the Graduate Programme, King's College, London, 2012-4.

Karla Dearsley

Karla Dearsley's stories, flash fiction and poetry have appeared online and in print on both sides of the Atlantic. When she is not writing, she lets her dogs take her for walks. She has a short story anthology available from Smashwords and a fantasy novel on Kindle. Find out more at http://www.ksdearsley.com.

Ruth Driscoll

Ruth Driscoll was born in South Wales and studied French & Spanish at Oxford University. She worked in overseas development for over a decade before choosing to stay at home with her three children in London and try her hand at creative writing.

Gerard Duffy

Born in Leicester, now living in Bristol, Gerard has written short stories for several years. He completed his first (as yet unpublished) novel whilst undertaking an MA in Creative Writing at Bath Spa University. He says, "Seeing one's work in print is the best possible reward." He is currently working on his second novel.

Gillian Dunstan

Gillian Dunstan was born in Somerset. She graduated in English from Southampton University and taught in secondary schools for many years. Although she has always enjoyed writing fiction, she only began to write poetry following her retirement. To date, she has won two poetry competitions and has been shortlisted in several others. Gillian lives with her husband in Devon and is a member of the Culm Valley Writers' Group.

Roger Elkin

Roger Elkin has won 45 First Prizes and several awards internationally, including the *Sylvia Plath Award for Poems about Women*, and the *Howard Sergeant Memorial Award for Services to Poetry* (1987*)*. His 10 collections include Fixing Things (2012); Marking Time (2012); and Bird in the Hand (2012). Editor of *Envoi*, (1991-2006), he is available for readings, workshops and poetry competition adjudication.

Suzanne Furness

Suzanne Furness lives in Cornwall with her husband, two daughters and a rather grumpy cat! She loves to write children's fantasy and is busy seeking publication for her series fiction. She finds that writing short stories for adults a welcome diversion from the unicorns and elves that normally fill her head. Visit her at suzannefurness.blogspot.co.uk

Judith Fursland

Much of Judith Fursland's poetry is inspired by nature and the nearby Quantock Hills. Animals on her smallholding also provide an endless source for writing.

Sandra Galton

Sandra Galton lives and works in London as a private piano teacher. She has recently taken up writing short stories and poems. Intrigued by the specular form used by Julia Copus to such good effect, this is Sandra's second specular poem.

Rose Garland

Rosie Garland has always been a cuckoo in the nest. She is an eclectic writer and performer and sings in post-punk band The March Violets. Her award-winning poetry has been widely published, including Mslexia, The Rialto and East Coast Literary Review. Her latest solo collection is 'Everything Must Go' (Holland Park Press). Her debut novel 'The Palace of Curiosities' won the Mslexia novel competition 2011 and was published by HarperCollins in March 2013. Her second novel, 'Vixen' came out in June 2014. http://www.rosiegarland.com/

David Grubb

David Grubb writes poems, short stories and novels. Recent poetry collections have been published by Salt, Shearsman and Like This Press. He runs a mentoring scheme for individuals writing fiction. His next poetry collection will appear in 2014.

Janet Hancock

Janet Hancock lives in Dorset and is her husband's carer and gardener-in-chief. Her short story *Memory* was published in *Dorset Voices* in 2012. Her completed novel *The Door of Darkness*, of which the opening chapter and synopsis won first prize at the 2011 Winchester Writers' Conference, was long listed in Mslexia's 2013 novel competition. She loves choral singing.

John Hargreaves

John Hargreaves reviews productions at his local theatre, is chair of governors at a local school, and was for a time head of communications at his local council – three interests which can all be seen at play in his short story Speak for Yourself, John. He has taught maths-for-welders in North Carolina prisons and helped women at HMP Drake Hall produce The Key – a magazine which won them numerous Koestler Awards (for creative writing in prisons). He has also worked as a freelance journalist and novelist.

Dennis Harkness

Dennis Harkness was once better known as Mr Brog, when for 25 years he toured Britain (and occasionally Europe) with his travelling solo puppet theatre. Now retired to Somerset, he writes a little and mows the lawn a lot. And daily walks the Quantocks with two border terrier bitches.

Bruce Harris

Bruce Harris began writing poetry and fiction after over thirty years in teaching and educational research, and became so consistently successful that in late 2013 his anthology of 25 stories which have all won prizes, commendations or listings in fiction competitions was published by SPM Publications: http://www.sentinelpoetry.org.uk/publications/first-flame Samples of his work can be seen at www.bruceharris.org

Claire Bugler Hewitt

Claire Bugler Hewitt grew up in East Coker and went to Yeovil's Preston Comprehensive and Yeovil College. She was a prizewinner in the Ian St James Awards and her haiku have been widely published in journals and anthologies. She lives in Dorset with her husband and two children, is revising her first novel and also writes short stories and letters of objection to Yeovil's Urban Extension Plan.

Sarah Hilary

Sarah Hilary's debut novel, Someone Else's Skin, is published by Headline in the UK, Penguin in the US, and in six other countries worldwide. A second book in the series will be published in 2015. Set in London, both books feature DI Marnie Rome. www.sarah-crawl-space.blogspot.co.uk/

Sandy Hogarth-Scott

Sandy Hogarth-Scott grew up in Australia. She has travelled widely, and lived and worked in Asia and mainland Europe. She gave up postgraduate teaching and research to write full time. She recently completed the UEA/Guardian Finishing a First Novel course and is now well into her second novel. She was commended for her short story, The

Boy, in the 2013 Yeovil Literary Prize. Sandy lives in Yorkshire with her partner but returns frequently to her roots in Australia. She is represented by Vivien Green at Sheil Land.

Christopher Holt

Christopher Holt was born in Devon but has spent much of his life overseas in Africa and Australia. He has worked as a teacher, broadcaster and field ecologist. At present he is working on his third novel.

Tracey Iceton

Tracey Iceton won the 2011 Writers Block NE Home Tomorrow Short Story Competition and the 2013 HISSAC short story prize for 'Butterfly Wings' and was shortlisted for the 2012 Bristol Short Story Competition with 'Apple Shot'. Her two novels have been long and shortlisted in the Bridge House Publishing Prize and the Cinnamon Press Debut Novel, Irish Novel Fair and Chapter One Children's Novel competitions. Her publication credits include; Prole, Litro, Neon, Tears in the Fence, Ride, The Yellow Room and the Brisbane Courier Mail. She is writing her third novel, book two of her trilogy on the Troubles in Ireland while preparing book one, Green Dawn at St Enda's, for publication by Cinnamon Press in early 2016. Her website is www.trywriting.co.uk and more information about her PhD research is available at:
www.northumbria.ac.uk/sd/academic/sass/about/humanities/englishhome/englresearch/pgresearchcw/traceyiceton11

Roger Iredale

Roger Iredale has published poetry since he was 18, and has appeared in many magazines, anthologies and frequently on BBC Radio 3. He is a winner of the Poetry Society's Greenwood Prize and the University of Reading's "Hurry" Medal for poetry. He recently won the Sherborne Festival poetry prize.

Sharon Keating

Sharon first entered a poem in the Yeovil Literary Prize in 2009 and was delighted when it achieved a Highly Commended from Carol Ann Duffy. Last year she had one short story published in *Aesthetica* and another shortlisted for the *Asham Award*. She lives in Brighton, just minutes from the sea.

Gill Le Serve

Now retired, Gill Le Serve spent many years teaching, mainly English as a Foreign Language to children and adults, in Europe and finally in Vietnam, which she says was a wonderful experience. The story 'A Stale Bun' was inspired by an advertisement in the paper for a charity caring for innocents caught in war zones. She now lives in New Zealand.

Carol Lovejoy Edwards

Carol Lovejoy Edwards has been writing all of her life but only recently taken it seriously. Aside from short stories she has written three novels and has a non-fiction book about her home town during World War One due out in the summer. She is currently researching her next non-fiction book.

Dru Marland

Dru Marland is a sometime mariner, now Bristol-based illustrator and aspiring poet, when she is not fixing bicycles and her Morris Traveller.

Patricia McCaw

After a long career in social work Patricia McCaw completed a Masters in Creative Writing degree at Edinburgh University, where she studied fiction, mainly. Her deepest love is poetry, and she buys as many poetry books as she can. Her own writing is strongly influenced by her Irish origins. She used to volunteer feeding gannets, seals, foxes and ferrets!

Elizabeth McLaren

Elizabeth McLaren was born in London but moved to the West Country as a child and now lives up on the Blackdown Hills. She was amazed and delighted when Lola came third in the Yeovil Literary Prize as she has only been writing for a short time and this is one of her first stories. With this as encouragement, hopefully, there will be more to come.

Kiran Millwood Hargrave

Kiran Millwood Hargrave was born in London in 1990. She is a Barbican Young Poet, and her third collection Splitfish was published by Gatehouse Press in 2013. Her poetry has appeared in magazines including Magma and Agenda. Kiran is undertaking an MA at Oxford

University, where she is President of the Oxford University Poetry Society. www.kiranmh.co.uk

Fiona Mitchell

Fiona Mitchell is a freelance features writer. In 2013, she completed her first novel and was shortlisted into the final three of the WowFactor competition run by literary talent spotters Cornerstones. That year, Fiona was also commended in the Yeovil Literary Prize. She is currently working on her second novel. Connect with her on Twitter @FionaMoMitchell

David Punter

David Punter lives and works in the Bristol area, and has published five books of poetry: *China and Glass*, *Asleep at the Wheel*, *Lost in the Supermarket*, the confusingly-titled *Selected Short Stories* and *Foreign Ministry*. With singer-songwriter Barry Hill and fellow-poet Ananda, he is part of the group Smoke and Mirrors, which has done many performances in the West Country.

Michael Roe

Michael is passionate about crime writing and political thrillers. After retiring early from a career in telecommunications he has devoted himself to the pain and pleasures of novel and short story writing. Born and raised in London he now lives in Dorset.

Emma Seaman

Emma Seaman has won prizes including the Wells Literary Festival and Jeremy Mogford awards for her short stories, as well as being published in seven anthologies in the UK and US. She is a marketing /social media professional and lives in Devon with her family. For more information about her writing, see www.emmaseaman.co.uk

Blanche Sears

Blanche Sears hails from the North East and spent schooldays scribbling poetry on bits of paper. She moved southwards for University and then on to London where she taught English to Secondary pupils. Married with three children she gains inspiration from belonging to a small Writing Group.

Marcus Smith

Marcus Smith is a current finalist for The Live Canon First Collection Competition. He has twice been a Cinnamon Press Finalist and twice shortlisted for The Bridport Prize.

Catherine Strong

Catherine Strong works as an editor and whale-watch tour leader for a wildlife travel company. 'Kangerlua' was inspired by a trip Catherine made to western Greenland in 2007. She also writes children's stories. When not writing she enjoys being with friends and family and playing with her ragdoll cat.

Chip Tolson

Architecture, National Service, international container and ship owning trades kept Chip busy before an MA in Creative Writing led him to the joy of short stories; success in the Yeovil Literary Prize has been a great encouragement. He has also written short plays and has two novels in want of a publisher.

Andrew Tomkinson

Andrew Tomkinson is a poet. He lives in Oxford. He spends his time writing poetry, often about Oxford, and author bios to accompany his poetry about Oxford which are even less interesting to read than his poetry about Oxford.

Louise Walford

Louise Wilford has had around 50 poems published in magazines including Agenda, Iota and Seam, and has won several poetry competitions. She has been long listed for both the National Poetry Competition and the Bridport Prize and has had a collection shortlisted for the Templar Poets pamphlet competition. She currently lives in Yorkshire where she teaches and is working on a fantasy novel.

Gillian Wallbanks

Gillian Wallbanks was delighted to win first prize for her short story in the Yeovil Literary Prize in 2011, and then to be highly commended in 2012. She has also had a story published in 'Writers Forum' magazine.

She writes Science Fiction and stories about social problems for a booklet produced for charity. Currently, she is writing the third book in a trilogy of crime novels. Gillian comments that she has burnt countless dinners whilst writing 'a few more lines!'

Alan Ward

Alan Ward is a writer based in London. He has poems, stories and articles published online and in print, most notably in Magma and Popshot magazines. In 2013 the London Canal Museum commissioned him to write a series of poems about ice. Find him on Twitter: @alan_john_ward

Louise Warren

Louise Warren's first collection 'A Child's Last Picture Book of the Zoo' won the Cinnamon First Collection Prize and was published in 2012. Her poems have appeared in Ambit, Agenda, Envoi, The Interpreters House, Fuselit, London Grip, Orbis, The New Writer, Obsessed with Pipework, Poetry Wales, The Rialto, South, Seam and Stand. In 2013 she was a Prizewinner in the Troubadour International Poetry Competition, highly commended in the Ver Prize and runner up in the Cinnamon Press Single Poem Competition.

Rowena Warwick

Rowena Warwick is a writer of poetry and fiction, currently on the University of Oxford's Undergraduate Diploma in Creative Writing. She lives near Oxford with her husband, sons and Westie and works for the health service.

Printed in Great Britain
by Amazon.co.uk, Ltd.,
Marston Gate.